ISBN: 9781290507516

Published by:
HardPress Publishing
8345 NW 66TH ST #2561
MIAMI FL 33166-2626

Email: info@hardpress.net
Web: http://www.hardpress.net

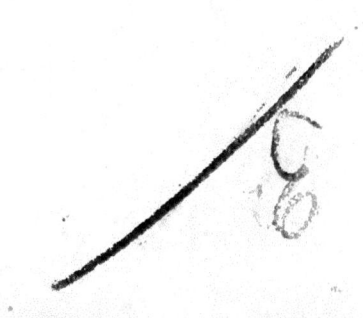

MAY FAIR.

IN FOUR CANTOS.

"I cannot suspect it in the man whom I esteem, that there is the least spur from spleen, or malevolence of intent in these sallies. I believe and know them to be truly honest and sportive:—but consider, my dear lad, that fools cannot distinguish this,—and that knaves will not." *Tristram Shandy*.

LONDON:
WILLIAM H. AINSWORTH,
OLD BOND STREET.
1827.

LONDON:
PRINTED BY S. AND R. BENTLEY, DORSET STREET.

CONTENTS.

	Page
THE MORNING VISIT.	3
THE DINNER.	61
THE AFTER-DINNER.	99
THE MIDNIGHT DRIVE.	141
L'ENVOY.	190

MAY FAIR.

CANTO I.

Trova prima il Silenzio, e da mia parte
Gli dì, che teco a quest' impresa venga.
Fornito questo, subito va in parte
Dove il suo seggio l'Amor tenga.

Orlando Furioso.

MAY FAIR.

CANTO I.

THE MORNING VISIT.

DEDICATION.

TO LORD H—OLLAND.

My Lord, whom all that know you know
The best good-natured man below;
With all of Fox's better part,
The vigorous head, the generous heart;
Who touch the point so hard to hit
'Twixt sportive sense and venom'd wit;

How often, in your evening chair,
I've seen your honest bosom bare;
When, circled by the chosen set,
Forgetting man was made to fret;
Glad as a schoolboy from his task,
You toss'd aside the day's dull mask;
Cared not a doit for all the din
Of Whig and Tory, out or in;
But as the glass its circuit ran,
Forgot the Statesman in the man:

Then, as the unsought memories rose,
Discuss'd the mighty in repose,
Or touch'd in smiles the stuff that passes
For wisdom in our world of asses;
Gave in your own unrivall'd way
The fierce formality of GREY;

Old Grenville's triple-sentenced talk,

Like skim-milk thicken'd up with chalk.

(Alike his Lordship's talk and tail

Descended to the nearest male.)

The nonsense Lord George gets by rote,

Fit preface to his annual vote.

Old Bags's glance of fear and wonder,

When out bursts L*******'s tide of blunder;

The conflict of the parts of speech,

When D******'rises—" to impeach :"*

That emblem of a worn-out rattle,

That stirs but never shares the battle.

---

* A great patriot and investigator of Admiralty atrocities; but rather fallen in his vigour. He has not of late demanded the head of Lord Melville, more than about once in every two years.

The true prize-oxen speech and look,
That shows us to the life—*the* Duke;
Or, giving all thy frolic swing,
Revived Joe Miller in Joe K * *. *. †
The sap-dried brain put out to nurse,
The pun for better or for worse;
The floundering tale, the desperate joke,
The economic plan of smoke,

---

† A most painstaking and praiseworthy jester. Nothing comes amiss to him more than to the Ostrich. Taxes, turnpike-bills, Chancery, civil-law, gas-light, and the circulating medium, all go down alike. Once taken into his gastric region, they all re-appear in the same shape,—a joke. He is the legitimate successor of Lord Stanhope, who, with a due sense of his merit, bequeathed to him his commonplace book. He wants nothing but that noble lord's memorable breeches to be " Stanhope himself again."

D. & W.

Till laughter half-convulsed the ring,
And, all but conscience, there sat K***.

Thus, admitted of thy crew,
Have I sat till midnight flew;
Those delights while thou canst give,
With thee, H*****d, will I live.
And with me among thy peers,
May'st thou live those thousand years!

Now, thou fattest, best of men,
Smile upon thy Poet's pen.

———

Reader, hear my mystery,—
No dabbler with the Muses I;—
No rambler o'er their hackney'd hill,
With all my rent-roll in my quill:

No brain-besieging monthly bore,
No working member of the corps,
I lounge along an easy life,
Untroubled with a muse or wife;
To all the wits I lightly yield
The glories of the paper field;
Not one among the diners out—
I neither mimic, sing, nor spout.*

---

* Very good persons they are that do all those things, and very much indebted should we be to them for their trouble. In fact, the hours of theatres and things of that sort are so preposterous, that we should never know any thing of them except for those gentlemen. They give us every thing good in those places, without compelling us to go to them. By one gentleman in particular, whose name has escaped my recollection, but who carries songs in

THE MORNING VISIT.

Without a sigh I leave old Frere,

To tell his stories once a year.

See Bobus Smith eternal planning,

To charm us second-hand with Canning.

No flutterer in the crowd of Blues,

I neither kiss their lips nor shoes.

In short, to set the thing at rest,

I live—wherever I live best:

I rise at two, am seen at four,

Once cab it round the ring; no more,

Merely to countenance the Park:

Just reach the Clarendon by dark.

---

his pocket, and 'is, to do him justice, very ready in their performance, I will acknowledge I have been considerably amused. S. R.

Content three times a week to dine
Wherever I approve the wine;
Nor wish the giver in the Styx,
Although his vulgar hour were six;
Nor give him my especial hate,
Although he should not feed off plate;
Nor think the thing the more inhuman,
If chequered tastefully with women:
Not *too much* wife, and *no* relations—
Those people never know their stations.

Dear to my soul art thou, MAY FAIR!
There Greatness breathes her native air
There Fashion in her glory sits,
Sole spot still unprofaned by Cits.
There all the mushroom, trading tribe
In vain would bully or would bribe:

THE MORNING VISIT.

The Rothschilds, Couttses, Goldsmids, Barings,
In other spots must have their pairings;
We fix your bounds, ye rich and silly,
Along the road by Piccadilly;
Convenient spot for the approaches
Of Cousins who keep hackney-coaches;
And duly, (if the Sunday's fine,)
Come down to pudding and port wine;
Or drop, like pigeons from a cage,
Six insides from the shilling stage.

Hail! seat of her that earliest stole *
Just half my heart and all my soul!

---

* The leader of every thing—party and partizans, pretty women,—and also of Whigs, that are any thing but pretty.

Thou realm of all my J~~ERSE~~y's glories,
Sovereign alike of Whigs and Tories!

Hail now, for time the tenth, MAY FAIR!*
Though many a stable scents thy air—

'Tis true, the Duchess of Devonshire was a leader, and even a leader of Whigs. But *then* a Whig might be a gentleman; and Charles Fox was certainly worth a woman's while. But these days are over.

* All the world knows, or should know, MAY FAIR— the *noble* quarter of London. The writers of Novels of Fashionable Life, a tribe who seem to have as much knowledge of that life as an Esquimaux has of pinks and pine-apples, class it under the " West End," and describe it in their eloquent and natural style as a region of palaces. Let such not be believed. The very term " West End" detects the *locale* of those high-bred

THE MORNING VISIT.

Though many a butcher's glowing shambles
Startle the beauty's morning rambles—
Though to her horror many a Jew
Shows her past stockings " goot as new"—
Though, swung from many a dyer's pole,
Old blankets catch her eye's blue roll;
And petticoats, in league with breeches,
Increase the atmospheric riches;
A sort of upper story bower
To filter the eternal shower;
And dropping down their dingy dew,
Veneer her skin with black and blue.

---

authors. The word is indigenous east of Temple Bar, flowers less profusely along the Strand, dies off in the neighbourhood of Charing Cross, and thenceforward becomes absolutely unknown.

Yet, land of *ponch romaine* and plate,

Of dinners fix'd at half-past eight;

Of morning lounge, of midnight rout,

Of debt and dun, of love and gout,

Of drowsy days, of brilliant nights,

Of dangerous eyes, of downright frights,

Of tables where old Sidney shines,*

Of ladies famous for their wines:

---

* A pleasant creature as lives; but now growing pursy and polemical to a painful degree. I remember to have been much amused with a version of a charge issued in, what he somewhere calls, " the vexatious bustle of a new Bishop." The foundling was, by the natural fate of a notorious *jeu-d'esprit* culprit, left at his door—perhaps, however, without any very exact enquiry into the relationship.

Grim Countesses that make their way—
Resistless charmers!—by Tokay;

My Reverend Brethren,
" Dance not, sing not, fiddle not, flute not;
Hunt not, fish not, course not, shoot not;
Bow down in the dust to all men with big wigs,
Whip your children betimes, and take care of your pigs;
Strip off all your trowsers; you know the Law teaches
The priest was no priest till he put on his breeches.
So henceforth, I hope, you'll eschew your *loose habits*,
And further attend to your tithe of the rabbits,
Likewise of the cabbages, corn, and potatoes,—
The farmers are always conspiring to cheat us.
Now, go home to your wives, nip iniquity budding,
Feed well when you can, but avoid too much pudding;

Of bold *on dit* and plain *soupçon*,
Known to all mankind but *the* one ;
Of tedious M. P.'s, pursy peers,
Illustrious for their length of ears ;
Of Dice and Doctors, Bowstreets Bards,
Crowds, Concerts, Chat, Champaigne, and Cards;
Of all the S-m-rs, Br-d-lls,—Br-ces,
The St-h-p-s, Pagets, Gowers, De-Roses ;
Of faction, flirting, and quadrille ;—
With all thy faults, I love thee still!

Keep your surplices clean, also cure your own bacon :—
The man who does these things can't be much mistaken.
On Sundays besides, 'tis my special desire
That, invited or not, you all dine with the Squire."

And, while I have a love to spare,
Dear to my soul art thou, MAY FAIR!

Take fifty of your modern bards—
(Your porter's sure to have their cards—
Alike to them the saint or sinner;
The true Amphitryon gives the dinner)—
I'll bet you fifty pounds a-piece
They plunge their pens at once in Greece;
No matter though the subject roam
Not half of fifty miles from home;
Some fact that lay before your eye:
Who last gave gallant B****** the lie:
Who, to the mirth of all beholders,
Last laid the switch across his shoulders;

Who last rubb'd up thy fur, my Horse,
In what Sir Francis calls " that room,"
And show'd the world its great debater
In every sense a *calculator*.
Not one of them could pen a line
With " sweet simplicity" like mine.

The point of points is to astonish;
Hyde Park and Hounslow turn Byronish;
If deuce a word you understand,
The Bard's the surer of the *grand*.
Out burst the Cerebellum's labours,—
A gush of pistols, poniards, sabres,
Mail, muskets, timbrels, Turkish tunes,
Drums, trumpets, full and half-full moons;
Mustachios, monks, pashas with three tails,-
You 'll have them all, in all the details;

With notes on Helicons, Apollos,
And so forth ;—all the rest that follows.

Then comes the Heroine, soul of feeling,
With passion, heavenly passion, reeling ;
Her eye all flash, her cheek all glow,
Her soul on fire from top to toe ;
Though lost, still loved, a glorious wreck,
Her thoughts as naked as her neck ;
Faults, follies, frailties, crimes, combine,
They make her but the more divine.
She robs, stabs, poisons,—but her tear,
Delicious drop ! makes all things clear.
And take your life, or take your purse,
My lady 's not a hair the worse.

I pledge myself to keep the peace—
May Fair shall be *my* only Greece.
One twinkle of young P—g—t's eyes,
Worth all the stars in all her skies;
Ladies and Loves, your poet's pen
Shall charm you but with Christian men,
No goblins worse than Brooks' or White's.
I scorn to give you nightmare nights;
I starve you on no Alpine tract;
I plunge you down no cataract;
(Grim forests all the skylight dimming—
Below, for life, the lady swimming;)
No sudden lava round you flashes,
Leaving the world a beauty's ashes;
No Rhenish eddy sucks you under,
To rise some fishy Dutchman's wonder;

THE MORNING VISIT.

You fill no wolf's luxurious paunch;
You freeze beneath no avalanche;
You see no storms in terror stalk;
You hear no hills in high Dutch talk;
When, 'by particular desire,'
Old Nick deserts his house of fire;
And, 'that night only,' plays his parts,
In his old Drury Lane, the Hartz;
While new-spread clouds on all the hills
Serve for the Roscius' posting-bills.

Then every necromantic burgess
Secures a seat for the Walpurgis;*

---

* The Walpurgis—the annual fête champetre of the German witches. Goethe has had the fortune to find an

With cloth of gold are lined the ditches,
Reserved for sixteen-quarter witches;
The lower on the sulphur roll,
With broad-cloth must their tails console.
Then every precipice's crupper
Sustains a' regular-bred supper.
There's not the most ill-featured rock
But has its compliment of hock;
There's not an oak dares show a branch
Without a sirloin or a haunch;
The peach hangs out among the brambles—
In short, it shames our May Fair scrambles!

English translator who has actually done him more justice than any or all of his translating hundreds or thousands in all the languages of Europe. For poetry and passion, Lord Gower's FAUST against the field!

THE MORNING VISIT.

(How oft, amid the dear five hundred,
I 've seen the struggling footman plundered—
Seen the orgeat by belles waylaid,
The war for life and limonade,
And not a sandwich left to tell
The fate that all its tribe befell.)
Then, while the moon above them halts,
Rings all the welkin with the waltz;
And every hill plays harp or horn
Till comes the hateful air of morn—
Its vulgar breath of pinks and roses
Offensive to their sulphur noses.
Each from her pocket plucks her salts
Each on her maneged broomstick vaults,
Settles her petticoats for flight,
And vows " a most delightful night!"

While, as he mounts his chaise of flame,
The master of the melodrame
Consigns it to the Earth below,
Aux soins de Goethe, Gower & Co.

At length comes out the virgin Spring,
Still under Winter's matron wing;
While storm and shower and sleet and dust,
Like Guardians, keep her still in trust.
Now all the Beau-monde wake together,
Like swallows at the change of weather;
The belles, blue, deep-blue, white and brown,*
Make up their minds and cheeks for town:

---

* There is a delicate distinction between the BLUE and the DEEP BLUE. The former merely reads Reviews, &c.; the latter writes them. The former merely falls in love

THE MORNING VISIT.

The young, the old, the wed, the single,
Feel through their veins the annual tingle.

All Peers with hosts of *second* sons,
All Baronets sick of rustic duns;
All M.P's. with unsettled votes,
Determined to new-line their coats;
All dames who, tired of pigeon-cooing,
Long to know what the world is doing;

---

with the works of poets, &c.; the latter falls in love with the poets, &c. in person. The former merely attends Albemarle-street, and is content to see Mr. Brande burn his own fingers, and singe his own minutely curled periwig. The latter practises the experimental philosophy at home, burns wig and fingers at her own expense, and blows up her husband and children. S. R.

All widows weary of their sable—
All mothers of the marriageable,
That, keen as bees about their honey,
Hunt every bush for man and money;
Spite of the wind's and rain's embargo,
Each coming with her native cargo.
First shown to the discerning few,
Like pictures at a private view;
All vulgar bidders being ejected
Until the 'gems' have been selected:
But, if no high-born pencil mark it,
The sample then must play and park it;
And have its texture and its tints,
Like Urling's lace and Howell's chintz,*

---

* Mr. Urling, the proprietor of the finest lace, and finest young gentlemen distributors of it, imaginable. The ele-

Displayed by the attendant matrons,

On Hymen's counter, the Spring patterns;

The blonde, the bronze—so much per set—

Each ticketed a coronet,

A jointure, pin-money; of course

A sum in case of a divorce—

(No age this of the flitch of bacon)—

Not five pounds under can be taken.

---

gance of their *coiffure* is really an honour to commerce, and a charming evidence of the advanced civilization of the 19th century and the counter. It is shop-keeping urged to the highest point of the curling-iron capacity. Worcester protests, that though his nature is not prone to envy, he hates to pass by the boudoir of those charming young persons. And Bankes, who has seen every kind of curl from the Iroquese to the Abyssinian, allows that he has seen " nothing like it," and sighs over the vanity of travel.

Sweet Spring! let bards of thorn and thistle
Tell the tired world how blackbirds whistle;
How rabbits at thy summons burrow—
How cackle hens, how ploughmen furrow;
How herd on herd of hunting squires
Play all the jackass, like their sires;
How maidens, at their suit made wives,
Repent it for their natural lives;
How, like a rogue fresh 'scaped from jail,
Limps Nature, ragged, squalid, pale,
Till her full feed of sun and air
Plumps up the thin, and clothes the bare.
Such topics fit the attic-lodgers—
I know no more of fields than Rogers.*

---

* " *Diseur de bons mots, mauvais caractère*, is the stern sentence of PASCAL, himself a deep *diseur*, and of course

Now Fashion's realm is all alive—
Ah, *très heureux celui qu'y vive*—
No more around the naked square
You send your desolated stare:
Lifeless, but where some half-pay sinner
Walks, when all Christians go to dinner;

---

acquainted with the criminality of the profession.—But it is not applicable in this instance. Rogers is of puns and points the *Chevalier sans peur et sans reproche*. He says *all* the good things. He has enjoyed this incomparable monopoly longer than an East India charter. The facetiæ are his by a sort of Parnassian act of Parliament; and the only *jeux-d'esprit* that have a chance of popularity must, like the " Widow Welch's pills," be issued under the popular name. His restless brilliancy in the Sunday newspapers is unrivalled and unrivalable. J. M.

No more along five miles of street
Rings the lone echo of your feet;
No more your half-reluctant knock
Sends round the square the sudden shock.
The startled porter in the hall,
Doubts whether 'tis a human call;
And from the window, on his guard,
Inspects you ere he takes your card.
The beadle stops to reconnoitre—
Thinks that he knows your easy loiter;
And marks you, as you tread the gravel,
An old offender come from travel.
The footman, from his area grate,
Swears that you have an eye to plate—
Deems your high air but more suspicious,
And hurries to lock-up his dishes.

Ecstatic change! the desert, den,
Is peopled; all May Fair again.
There, by the pendule half-past three,
Rolls out the *well-known* vis-a-vis.
None ever bore a lovelier freight
Than thee, my folly and my fate—
Thee, from whose eyes the slightest glance
Can make the very life-blood dance;
Whose smile can all the spirit seize,
Do all but set the heart at ease!
There mutual stanhopes—stanhopes meet;
There totter belles on Chinese feet;
There beauty half her glory veils
In cabs, those gondolas on wheels;
There shakes the pavement the barouche;
There rides my lord *en Scaramouche;*

There through the gay confusion dashes
The Lancer, man of spurs and sashes;
There footmen lounging by the score,
Stand, decorations of the door:
Your only dressers, costly beaux,
As well his Lordship's rental knows.

On sweeps your cab—you make your calls:
Sow cards, broad-cast, the seed of balls;
For, if through life you'd take your fling,
A pasteboard friendship's just the thing.
'Tis quick to make, 'tis cheap to keep,
Its loss will never break your sleep;
It gives your friend no right to borrow—
If ruined, you cut him dead to-morrow.
You hear the Duchess is done up—
You cast about where next to sup:

You hear the Viscount's dead, or worse—
Has run his mortgage length of purse;
My Lady from my Lord revolted,—
In short, the whole concern has bolted;
Yet you 're no party in the quarrel,
In which you 're sure to gain no laurel;
And though you grieve the house is dish'd,
Where twice a-week you soup'd and fish'd;
Yet, being neither aunt nor mother,
You drop your pasteboard with another.

Now to the Marchioness I drive:
I find her rising—just alive;
Exhausted by the last night's rout—
The spirits in her lamp burnt out;

Upon her visage I inspect
Three balls, two suppers " most select."
The shaking of her hand of snow
Still seems to meditate *the* throw :
I read upon her dazzling forehead
The very last rouleau she borrow'd.

Ye weary washers of chemises ;
Ye warm artificers of cheeses ;
Ye ploughmen's ladies, who must wake,
Before the dawn, to brew and bake ;
Ye milkmaids, who your charms display,
Piled overhead with curds and whey ;
Ye who with cobwebs wage the war,
Kneel down and thank your lucky star !
For press, or wash, or milk, or sweep,
Still, spite of fortune, you can *sleep*.

No rabble roar, no strife of poles,
Disturbs your linsey-wolsey souls;
No Brussels drapery gone to wreck,
Gives to the world your knee or neck.
The midnight o'er your blanket flies;
The morn is up, you rub your eyes;
Then off to milk, sweep, wash, and press,
Without a wrinkle more or less.

Around the fainting beauty glows
The boudoir silk, *couleur de rose;*
For, ladies' faces freshly made
By instinct cultivate the shade.
All belles of ton, 'twixt you and I,
Of noonday suns are somewhat shy—

Perhaps in pity to mankind,
Lest too much radiance strike you blind;
Perhaps because two suns together
Might make it rather sultry weather;
Perhaps because their brighter face
Might show Apollo's in disgrace;
Perhaps because the last night's rouge
Has left its blessing in gambouge.

In pour the crowd, a lovely mob,
Gay plunderers, careless whom they rob;
There L-mb-t's eyes of liquid black
Make on the soul a fierce attack;
There the last fragment of your freedom
Is prize to thy twin sapphires, N———m;
There the last scruple of your heart
Yields to thy white arm, B-u D-s-r-t;

THE MORNING VISIT. 37

There roams the eloquent and crazy,
Who sets her cap at Esterhazy;*
There she, whose conquering pair of blushes
Upset the Lord of all the Russias;
There she who, frigid below zero,
Yet leads in chains our modern Hero;
There she—La Grande de l'Embassade,
Soft as the pastures of Belgrade;
There she, who, two feet nigher heaven,
Gives heirs and happiness to Lieven;

---

* I rather think that thing's off a good deal. The little Hungarian is cunning; and, since the decline of *our* noble relations, is much more philosophical than he was a week before. Could he have expected any state secrets? The subject is curious, and I shall set it down in my tablets. L. S.

And she whose coy espiegle look
Wrought miracles—inspired the Duke;
When writing billet-doux with gas,
He " told his love" on window-glass.
Who the dear modesty can blame
That show'd his fondness by his *flame*,—
Kept all his blushes hid in night,
Yet gave his secret soul to *light*,
Till every mother thought *her* Emma
Had brought him to the true dilemma;
And, as the Rogers pours the strain,
All read their pleasure in his *pane?*

Let moralists say what they will,
They'll never make the world stand still.
If eyes are made the soul to pierce,
You'll have them at their carte and tierce:

If Nature whispers them, " Be killing,"
Manslaughter is but law-fulfilling.
Thus circled, by the deadliest belles,
I never try to break their spells.
By Cupid's shots eternal mangled,
Am thirty times a month entangled;
And though by mamma s under ban,
That blacksheep " not a marrying man,"
The first bright eye that says " Deliver!"
Has all the heart I have to give her.

Woe to the gay *celibataire*,
At whom are levelled Graville's pair!
No more in single blessedness
He wines it at the Knightsbridge mess;
No more his tumbril stops the way
Where Fashion throngs to see Perlet;

He droops, neglects his tailor, dreams;
Talks pastoral, writes verse by reams;
Looks low in chintuft and moustache;
Thinks cards a bore, and hazard rash;
Cuts all his well-dressed friends, grows mulish
In fact, plays to the life the foolish.
You'll see the hero on his rounds,
Although the dinner-bugle sounds;
Developing with double spine
The minnows of the Serpentine
And sullen, as if Earth forgot him,
Bespeaking lodgings at the bottom.
At length (for water spoils the figure)
He takes a fancy to the trigger,
Sits gravely down to make his will,
Feels, when 'tis done, he's living still;

Thinks marriage easier of digestion—
Dresses, drives out, and pops the question!

Round goes the chat,—the Rogers tells,
" No music like a ring of Belles;"
Deliciously the measure varies—
Who loves, who hates, who fights, who marries.
—" Heavens! how the Duchess lost at cards!
The money was of course her ward's."
" How the dear Viscount *will* be miss'd!
But yesterday the hands were kiss'd;
Some horrid place, Fate knows how far off,
Is always sure to take our star off:
The man who dances à merveille
Is certain to be first to sail."
—" Delightful opera, that La Gazza,
With Ayton playing the Ragazza,

Fine figure as she steals the spoons
To that most exquisite of tunes."
—" But Toso—ah, *superbe sensation !**
That *prima donna* importation"—
" Too much at once—youth, voice, and beauty ;
True Roman,—' pupil of Velluti.' "
" What think you, Colonel, of her eye ?"
" Oh, magnifique !—quite look and die.
I envy from my soul her *sposo !*
Ah ' Idol del mio core,' Toso !
" She 'll be a first rate hit for Ebers."†
—" So, M-o-o-re has melodramed the Ghebers ;

---

* A remarkably fine creature ; a noble figure, and one of the most promising voices that has caught the public ear for a long time. She is a prodigious favourite. W.

† The present proprietor of the King's Theatre, a very

The scenery all of Amh-e-rst's sketching—
The various forms of fever-catching;
The British style of marsh-encamping;
The Indian style of army-swamping;—
In short, you have before you set,
Au vif, a whole Rangoon Gazette."

" They say, the Bard, delicious treble,
You've heard, of course, his *chansons rebelles*,
Scorning to mix his pretty verses
(As odd as harlequins in hearses)

---

active, intelligent, and attentive administrator of that usually perplexed government. He has infinitely improved the performances, and, of course, the popularity of the Italian Opera. H. S.

With that infinitude of prosing,
That sets our whole seven senses dozing,
In all the regicide reviews;
Has put new stockings on his muse!
Thinks that the sight of loaves and fishes
Would decorate a poet's dishes;
In sundry paragraphs and rhymes
Is feeling out his way *by Times:*
Nay, R-g-rs swears, *has* joined the Tories,
And sighs,—*Oh tempora! Oh mores!* *

"So, W⁂ ⁂⁂⁂⁂⁂ and his wife have parted,'
"Yes, both the *lovers* broken-hearted."

---

    * Eheu *quo* fugit.—
       Qui spirabat amores
       Et me serpuerat mihi.

" *Fi donc*, my Lord —affairs of state,"
" *Ah, qu'oui*, the labours of debate,
When love had given the reins to reason."
" A mere arrangement for the season:
Her Father Jesuit, in a panic,
Thought the dear M-rq-s puritanic;
Felt certain controversial qualms,
Stirr'd by his style of singing psalms;
And, full of faith in salt and water,
Whisk'd over seas his failing daughter."

" You've heard the crash;— last night's breakdown?"
" Yes; that the Colonel's somewhat blown."
" Blown up;—the minor Lord was bubbled."
" Ten thousand?"—" Ay, twice that twice doubled.

" The Captain's done.—My Lord's attorney
Has hired one Scarlet and one Gurney."

" The Dowager's?"—" The Sunday party,
A Waltz, a Concert, and Ecarté;
It takes—the whole live world are there:
I never get beyond the stair."
" *Traitre,* you volunteer the station."
" Why, '*tis* convenient for flirtation:
There, like an angler on his weir,
One chooses from the ascending fair;
Or, like the sportsman, pulls the string
And nets the covey in its spring.
There, as the crowd sets strongly in,
Scarce thinking suicide a sin—
(The rooms your true Calcutta heat,
Thermometer at ninety-eight)—

When stript of silk, and ript of lace,
Crushes your ribs some battling Grace;
Or, hung upon your back, some nymph
Half melts into her native lymph;—
When, not to your expiring prayer
Your dearest friend would lend her chair.
Not wishing to depart this life,
I take some widow, maid, or wife,
And, perch'd among the staircase blooms,
Eschew the distant war of plumes;
Or, nestling in the boudoir window,
Watch *coolly* what the world within do."
" And try on all the self-same glances?"
" Why, that's *selon les circonstances*."
" If maid?"—" I look the sentimental!"
" First having ascertained her rental:"

MAY FAIR.

"Show her the moonlight through the trees;
Let on her cheek the garden breeze;
Talk Petrarch, troubadours, guitars,
Crusaders, Shakspeare, streams, and stars."
"If widow?"—"Satirize her set—
Her secret soul will pay the debt."
"If wife."—"Fill both her ears with scandal:
Her husband furnishing the handle!"

"The Duke not married!"—"Nor will ever;
He thinks the ladies much too clever!"
"'Tis pity—handsome, showy, young,
And, 'pon my life, he *has* a tongue!
His Thursday evenings *so* select—
I'll live to see him yet henpeck'd.
No Duke must drone it in our hive."
"The girl's not born that he will wive.

Though hundreds, M⸺, L ⸺, and H⸺,
Strive his philosophy to unlock ;
Though all the speculating mothers,
Have put themselves in various pothers,
And, spite of his Spitzbergen looks,
Still set their hearts on little Dukes ;
Cool as his favourite limonade,
He smiles on mother and on maid—
A frozen Anti-Benedict !"

" My word upon it, he 'll be trick'd ;—
Nay, if *I* thought it worth my while—"
" You'd make him any thing but smile.
Ay—torture, teaze, and tantalize ;
I *know* the power of those bright eyes ;
Round all his haughty spirit twine,
And make his chains—as charmed as mine !"

" Ah wretch ! you *know* I hate this talk,
So very *à la* moonlight walk."
" If thoughts as fond as ever vow'd,"—
" My Lord, pray recollect the crowd :
Truth is, those noble waifs and strays
Are open in a thousand ways :
Let but *the* one but smile her wishes,
All 's over with the Cavend—ish's !"
" What ! not one look—one last, kind word ?"
" Oh, hang it ! you grow quite absurd ;
And that old monster's eye insidious,—
To-day particularly hideous !—
Seems hearing every word you say ;
Begone ! the duchess gives a play ;—
La Porte, St. Ange, and all the rest :—
Those things are growing quite a pest !"

" There may I venture to encroach?"
" You'll do to hand us from our coach:"
" Till then, farewell! (there goes my Juliet)
Farewell! (I'll make *you* play the fool yet.)"

" The Colonel taken to the Quakers?"
" Yes,—housed in his paternal acres;
The club turned off—the hounds; the stud,
Et cetera—all the bits of blood!
The Plough unhorsed, the Star put out,
All Cheltenham to the right about!
No more delighting in fox-slaughter,
His *Vin de Comète* changed for water;
His field artillery, stock and rammer,
Knock'd up by Christie's knock-down hammer!

His table captains all dismist—
Grand clearance of his civil-list;
No word escapes his lips converted,
Without an oh! or ah! inserted;
Of G-rn-y the enraptured scholar,
He strips his coat of cuff and collar;
Shaves off his grooms the worldly locks,
Unpleasing to his Saint, George Fox;
Clothes all their sinful souls in drab—
The household of Aminidab;
Cuts up his mutton with a sigh,
And lives by leave of Sister Fry."

" A message!—Ay the old shake-hands
The game of questions and commands;
A drive to take a morning whet,
Then *déjeûner à la fourchette.*"

" No, faith ! a genuine thing—they fought :
I rode just now to see the spot.
The whole in form—Sir Bob, a surgeon ;
Sir Ronald, and a—' Major Sturgeon !'
Six rounds ! six paces—action hot !"
" I'll eat whichever one was shot."
" The battle early ; quite a by-way ;"
" Yes : noon, upon the Hounslow highway."
" 'Tis true—the thing was *rather* known."
" Right ! public men are not their own :
And, whether give or take their wounds,
Should war alone on *public grounds.*"
" SPRING-SOUP had caught"—"Or, got a hint—
That patriot who but lives in print ;—
That meteor of the Irish Whigs,—
That gentleman, who deals in figs ;

Who, now that N-w-p-rt gets the quinsy,
With " Emerald Isle," and so forth, dins ye;
Gives you at second-hand the tropes
Of her incarcerated *hopes;*
And looks the look, and groans the groan,
Of her much-injured, long-hang'd TONE!
" SPRING-SOUP, the best man at a rub,—"
" Established runner of the club,—"
" Flew off full speed to bring the bows;—"
" The rest the world of laughers knows."

Long may he live, and they to tell it,
Unsliced by crab-stick, steel, or pellet!
Long may their heirs desire their shoes!
Long may they scribble their reviews!
Long may their brains and boxes rattle!
Long may they wage the bloodless battle!

THE MORNING VISIT.   55

Sooner may Hymen raise a furrow
Beneath thy ringlets, Ellenboro';
Or —— scorn to bow the knee
To thee, illustrious lord in *fee;*
Or flesh disguise the charger's bones,
That stalks thee o'er the London stones.—
Sooner the little M-rch—n-ess
Be more adored, be talk'd of less;
Or watch her truant Lord's *démarches,*
Unaided by the DEAN of ARCHES —
Or Cowper lock her Opera-box,
On hearing my Lord Marshal's knocks;
While, conscious that his reign is done,
Sulks through the evening Palmersten.—
Sooner old Temple look the Duke,
Or bookworm Spencer read a book;

MAY FAIR.

Clerk Stan-hope learn his shirt to button;
Bedford talk any thing but mutton.
Sooner may shave Northumbria's Grace,
Than living man twit Raikes's face;
Sooner write *poetry*, Stewart Rose,
Than living man pull Sweepum's nose.

" A marriage?"—Yes, the fact's undoubted.
What, if my Lady Duchess pouted?--
So lovely, young, an angel voice!
By Jove, I envy him his choice!
What care I for a high-born fright?
No right like Beauty's sovereign right!
His whole long line not fit to wait on
The half of half your charms, my Paton.
Give *me* the lovely heraldries
Of ruby lips and sunny eyes;

No nobler *shield* than Nature's charms—
No *arms,* than two such snowy arms.
What care I where the blushing rose,
That wraps my sense in sweetness, grows?
What care I where the dark eye's blaze
That lights my soul, first shot its rays?
What care I in what sullen mine
My diamond first began to shine?—
Once master of her noble heart,
Against the world I 'd take her part;
And in a cot, or on a throne,
I 'd own her—and be proud to own.

END OF CANTO I.

MAY FAIR.

CANTO II.

Se Amante ancor tu sei
Come trovar sì poco
Sai negli sguardi miei
Quel ch'io non posso dir!
Io, che nel tuo bel foco
Sempre fedel m'accendo,
Mille segreti intendo,
Cara, da un tuo sospir.
    ATTILIO REGOLO.—METAST.

MAY FAIR.

CANTO II.

THE DINNER.

DEDICATED

TO LADY JERSEY.

When Venus gave your Ladyship
The red reversion of her lip,
And said, departing for the skies,
" Be magic in its smiles and sighs;"
And to your eye the glances lent,
Blue as her bluest element;

MAY FAIR.

And round you breathed the *Je ne scai quoi*,
That wins, yet keeps us all in awe ;—
I can't but think 'twas her intention,
In giving you this Venus-pension—
This ribbon of the Venus-garter,
To renovate sweet woman's charter—
Teach her to twist us like her glove,
Nay, though our wife, be still our love.

' . . . ,
But R–g–rs says, the rub of rubs,
Is QUEEN of *Hearts* turned QUEEN of *Club*
Beau Sexe, from soft fifteen to fifty—
No matter with what tongues Heaven gift y
Keep to your own delightful tricks,
And leave us port and politics.

THE DINNER.

When Beauty mounts the party-frown,
I write it—"conscious going down."
She whispers how the question goes;
My tablets bear it—"Ruby nose."
She sports a sarcasm on the King:
My tablets—"Cupid's on the wing."

'Tis Nature takes the loyal part;—
No woman ere was Whig at heart.
There never moved on earth a beauty,
But would have mankind kiss her shoe-tie.
The hideous may die *Democrate*—
The pretty rebel 's sure to rat:
If single, the sweet Radical
Would fling her fetter on us all;
If wedded, ask the lady's spouse,
Who has the right hand of the house.

In soul, all are, or would be, Queens,—
(You see I've peep'd behind the scenes.)

Even thou, by whose provoking tongue
Those dreary Whigs have lived so long;
Thy high-born look, thy polish'd wit,
Proclaim thee all, all hypocrite.
That wit, which from thy stately lip
Comes like a shaft with golden tip;
That look, which, spite of all thy art,
Proclaims thee *despot* of the heart;—
Nay, not a passing glance of thine
But flashes with the " Right Divine."

" Oh! woman, in our hours of ease,"
Who canst do any thing—but tease;

Make winter summer, and what not,
You'll find it all set down in Scott;
Canst charm alike the prince and peasant—
Nay, *almost* make the country pleasant;
Though, there to wind *me* up to bliss,
Would take a most uncommon Miss.

Preserve me! from the shapes that stalk
In memory round a village walk;
The Doctor, with his last year's news,
Tithes, turnpikes, politics, and pews;
Death's deputy, the Æsculapius,
Telling who last has got his *capias*,
The solemn Chairman of the Sessions,
Doling out knaves' and fools' confessions;

And, bitterest pill of all the three,
That bore of bores, the ex-M.P.

A Cato in his climacteric,
Making my very soul hysteric;
Your genuine Reminiscent, full
Of all that dullest makes the dull;
The stuff that time in pity stifles,—
The trifles—nay, the shade of trifles;
The stalest of the stalest stories,
Of long forgotten Whigs and Tories;
Embalming in his sexton-prose
The colour of their wigs and clothes;
The tedious twaddle of a brain,
Flat as his own homebrew'd champagne.

Oh! woman!—but " of this too much,"

May I be doom'd to hear High Dutch—

Or sit beside a Portuguese,

When summer sets her at her ease;

Or dine in presence of a wit,

In tortures till he makes a hit;

Or meet the T-mpl-s, sons or brothers—

Or see *my* flirt look soft on others—

Or listen to a Hume oration—

Or travel *Sec de la legation.*

Le Diplomat, ecstatic fate

Of the fifth cousins of the great:

Blest with a pound a-day for life,

To lacquey *Monsieur L'Envoy's* wife—

Teach French and figures to the daughter
See that they swallow their Spa-waters;
Prepared to answer every question
Touching your " sweet *eleve's*" digestion;
Take passport-pictures of the mob,
Who ramble to be robb'd, or rob;
The length of chin, the tint of nose,
The holes in breeches, and in hose.
Scribble the rout and dinner packs,
Lock up the royal pounce and wax;
Echo his Excellency's jest,
Mend your own stockings like the rest;
Dine how and where *il plait aux cieux*,
Battle his mongrel household crew;
Cook up his *cottlette* at a spirt,
Air *mi Lor's* newspaper and shirt,

Feel laugh'd, at by the luckier fribbles,
Till life between your fingers dribbles;
Condemn'd, till its last sands are roll'd,
To fold and frank, and frank and fold;
And envying every wretch in fetters,
Die as you've lived—a man of *letters*.*

---

* In my travels through the greater part of the habitable globe, Turkey, Wiltshire, Venice, and the Essex-fens, the Ukraine, and Whitechapel, I have never met with any thing, I pledge myself, as a man of honour, as an Irishman, as a Baron of England, and member of Brooks's, at once so useless, impudent, and miserable, as the whole minor diplomacy—the whole race of the *attachés* of this great and unfortunate country on the Continent. Playing the guitar, patching their own coats, terrifying the ears of foreigners of all descriptions with the guiltiest perversion of grammar, are fair enough

May I be doom'd to all: or worse,

Meet Grosvenor without length of purse; *

Without a peerage cross thy way,

Patrician of patricians—Grey.†

---

employments for the intellects of nine-tenths of them. But the three hundred and sixty-five pounds British, so expended annually, is one of the monstrous abuses of a state of things, in all its parts equally unnatural, improvident, unprincipled, and rushing to its speedy national ruin. I have been predicting the catastrophe every day these forty years. It must come!—It is coming! It has come! *Tout est perdu.* Take my word for it, so Vivent les Vauriens. (D——n.)

* The greatest brick-maker in the known world, and worth—what, I don't presume to say; probably, twice as much even as Prince Leopold has saved out of his ANNUITY!

† The fact notorious. Every one that knows me, knows

Or take on winter days thy hand,

Grim king of kelp, coals, salt, and sand.

Or hear stern G-nv-lle from his chair,*

Lash the low time-servers that *were;*

---

that I am not in the habit of retailing dinner anecdotes. Though, upon my life, *these* are not likely to have my Lord G—— for their hero. But the fact is, that no man in St. James's-street is more serviceable to save one's expenditure on ices in the dog-days; his very look is a Refrigerator. But from November to May—Heavens!—The other day I met little M—l Angelo, with his hand stuffed into his mouth: "Studying a new stew?" said I.—"Confound Grey," was the answer, "I just shook him by those icicles of his; and may I never mix lobster sallad again, but I am frostnipped for life."—W.

* I protest against this. If my lord did keep his place,

The slaves, that when their master's bank
Was cashless, with him feebly sank.
Unlike the generous friend of Pitt,
Who scorn'd his ancient Bench to quit,
Through patriot, pure distrust of Fox;
Still grasp'd the nation's money-box,
Stared vulgar scoffers in the face,
And kept his principles—and place.

---

what was it but common gratitude, for his place kept him? If he took office under Fox, what can be more proper than to be friends with all sorts of men? If he found himself the inspector of his own office, who could know more of his conduct than himself? Every man is the best judge of his own actions. I look upon him as a model for statesmen, who deserve to be remembered by their *families.* N.

THE DINNER.

May I be shot! nay sent to singe a
Conscience and cuticle in India;
Dispute Sir James's dinner *dictum*,
To die of Scotch and snuff the victim;
Turn from Mt. Charles's rosiest *oscolo*;
Sit out a mortal hour of F-sc-lo,
(With all the prosing *post* and *ante*
That prosers ever prosed of Dante)
Nay, be thy rival, Signor Torri —
Ere make a woman sad or sorry!

What! she, whom all my summer days
I've worshipp'd with all sorts of lays;
She, on whose smiles my boyhood hung!
Whose glance alone now tunes my tongue;
Sting *her!* I could not if I dared,
The thought would all unbard the Bard.

The poison on her soul distil!
My hand at once would lose its skill;
My Cupid moult his purple wing,
My lute instinctive break the string;
And giving to the winds its moan,
Lament its noblest spirit gone.

No!—Let the tribe who daily dabble
In all the stuff call'd—fashionable.*

---

* Peevish! Peevish! Peevish! I join in no general charge against any man or set of men. The works are admirable in every sense of the word. Admirable for fancy; for the writers never can have seen what they describe. Admirable for research; for they have evidently pressed every page of M. Ude and his co-adjutors in their own; and admirable for the perfect originality of their

Knowing as much about the matter
As their own shoemaker and hatter;
To raise the laugh of tradesmen's wives,
Discuss, Heaven help us! noble lives—
No! trust *my* page, a woman's tear
Shall never drop in anguish here:

---

conceptions of good society, for they have absolutely created a new species of its existence. I understand, from my publisher, that those works are growing into rapid request in Australia; that the Don Cossacks take a vast number; and that in the Illinois and Otahéite, they are rapidly promoting cookery and civilization. In my next edition of my Poems, I intend to make honourable mention of what I look on, as, upon the honour of a legitimate, popular, and immortal poet, a very great accession to the culinary Cause, in our day of steam ranges and science at sixpence a-head. S. R.

Rather for life I'd burn my pen,
Than be the man, the shame of men;
The assassin scribbler of a line,
That made the cheek of beauty pine.

'Tis dinner! silence all, and state,
Long footmen, peeresses, and plate,
A sprinkling of the Guards—some lovers,—
My memory fails me in the covers—
I leave them to those—gentlemen,—
Who wield the "fashionable" pen;
Historiographers of pies,
Who lay the *carte* before your eyes.
Adepts in all the tribes of jelly,
The very toughest names they'll spell ye,
Through all the pâté-climax soar,
From *poisson* up to *perigord*;

Or stretching still a higher strain,
Touch the *rognons a la champagne.*
Then, as their loftier genius shines,
Amaze your feelings with the wines!
The St. Peray, La fitte—Lunelle,
You'd think the *bouquet* meets your smell!
La Rose, Leoville, Latour, Preignac,
You'd swear you had them at your back!
The *Sillery*, cool, delicious, still,
You feel your whole machinery thrill!
The pink champagne, rich, creamy, sparkling,
You see the room around you darkling!
The king of cups, the *grande* Bourgogne,
You feel your whole seven senses gone!
Though says the Rogers, at *his* age
He'd like a little *Hermitage.*

But others, the superior works,
Give you exact the spoons and forks,
So that if spoon or fork be miss'd,
The butler buys them for a list.
Nay others, abler than them both,
Square-inch the table and the cloth;
(Of Algebra the fine appliance,
The modern, mighty march of science!)
Tell you how many off them dined;
How many valets stood behind,
How many buttons on their coats,
How many sauce-and-butter boats;
How many fair ones fill'd their glasses,
Who bumpers it! who sips, who passes!-
Long live!—ye wonder working works,
Where something for all *palates* lurks,—

THE DINNER.

For sixpence, where the hungry sinner,
Miss what he may, will find a *dinner*.
And all, from footmen up to cooks,
Own you the very books of books!

The Chaplain sends his whisper round :
Then follows much more *sense* than sound ;
For who, above an Esquimaux,
Would speak till the *Entrée s* withdraw ?
What mortal that pretends to taste,
Would see such moments run to waste ?
Till, with the lighter *entremets*
The *business* lessens by degrees.
Then whispers wake !—a dropping fire,
That seems to near you, then expire ;
A kind of conversation-ague,
That comes at intervals to plague you ;

Instalments of a debt of tongue,
You wish the caller for it hung:
A tardy, intermittent talk,
Like watchmen on their midnight walk,
Just venturing from their wooden den,
To growl, and be ensconced again.
Then, as the wine its circuit goes,
We start upon the native prose;
The atmospheric Conversation
Dear to our weather-beaten nation.
" Fine morning,—stormy—sunshine—cloudy—
So cold, scarce gave her grace a how-d'ye;—
The park hot—damp—dry—rainy—fine—
Calm—windy—honor to take wine;
Sharp breeze; Lord Duke—Tokay?"—" With pleasure."
Till of his neighbour each takes measure;

No doubt we thus escape High Treason,—
In England all things have a reason.

Before he *opens*—thus the hound
Maps with his cautious nose the ground.

Thus, your established man of jest,
Dreading to lose his *very best*,
His way by inuendo tries
Before he makes the grand *surprize*.

Thus, thieves their optics round them dart,
Ere from their holes they make the start.

Thus, Normanby his novel writes,
To set "the matter" in all lights;

Deeming, in *rebus* yet *intactis*,
His theory should precede his practice.

Thus soldiers ere they bivouac,
Probe all the corners of attack.

Thus B******* play'd the ultra-tory,
Before he plunged in papist glory.

Thus felons scorn to rest their toes
Upon the rungs by which they rose;
Heroic from the ladder spring,
And take their *independent* swing.

Thus the spruce scribes of high-life novels
First study fashion in their hovels;

Then licensed of the servant's hall,
Biographize us one and all.

Thus H̶u̶m̶e̶, a Greek among the Greeks,
First for his jobbing thousands seeks;
Then to the Greek appends the Jew,
And squeezes out, pounds fifty-two.

Thus D̶a̶v̶i̶e̶s̶, much renown'd for brain,
Talks stuff,—then rises to explain.

Thus B̶u̶x̶t̶o̶n̶, lord of vat and vapour,
Experiments his speech on paper;
Till on the all-important night,
He scrubs the Ethiopian white!

The R*g*rs says, that no man *hops*,
More pleasantly from psalms to slops;
No Saint that treads this wicked sphere
Thinks more devoutly of his *beer*.

Thus G****** shows the *Irish gag*,
Ere G-ulb-rn o'er the coals he drag.

Thus, like a Methodist in pain,
Ward plays the pious in Tremaine;
Finds out the swallow of the Town,
Then crams the politician down.

Thus patriots are to Newgate sent,
Academy for Parliament.
The R*g*rs says, " for party war
There 's no such training as the *bar* "

THE DINNER.   85

Thus lovers try the Lady's temper,
Before they make her *eadem semper.*

Thus, when you ballast a balloon,
With its two madmen for the moon,
The pilot-bladder mounts in token,
Which way their necks may best be broken.

Thus, ere he wields the nation's fates,
Lord John shows off on turnpike gates.

Thus one fair S̶m̶i̶t̶h, uxorious W̶o̶r̶c̶e̶s̶t̶e̶r̶,
Prepares your ring for all the cluster.

Thus Tierney cautious in his wrath
First tosses Br——m in C-nn-g's path.

Thus Irish rebels flog their cattle,
True patriots, foremost into battle;
And by the sacrifice of pigs,
Save for the world the breed of Whigs.

Thus all your new Administrations
Launch out inaugural orations;
" Grand era—Empire—noble scope—
Wealth—Habeas Corpus—saving hope!"
They never on essentials touch,
Until they have you in their clutch;
Then comes the Budget cent. per cent.,
Perhaps 'twill tell you what they meant.

The ladies gone, those dear *removes*,
Compote of sugar plums and doves!

THE DINNER.

The marquis on the throne vacated;
Our anguish partially abated:
For though, I own, the sex's presence
Is of life's essences the essence;
And though the last that leaves the room,
Dips every chandelier in gloom;
Yet, with our souls all cloth'd in sable,
We 're bound to rally round the table;
In the most desperate condition,
Renew our claret ammunition;
Mourning our decimated ranks,
Feel up like soldiers, from the flanks;
And try the battle to sustain,
By new discharges of Champagne.

Now comes *the* hour of English talk,
When no man will his subject balk.

MAY FAIR.

"Return'd from Greece?—The Capitani
Laughed at them, zany after zany;
In vain our patriots raved and rambled,
In dunghills sank—through thistles scrambled!
Ate cats,—in classic sludge bivouack'd,
Drank ditches,—baretailed rode bareback'd.
At sight or shadow of a Turk,
Felt as if swallowing his dirk!
Were flea-bit, dexter and sinister,
Till the whole patriot was a blister;
Were stript, and whipt, and sconced, and starved
Too happy to escape uncarved!

"Still, spite of all their English-Greek,
The Capitani "chewed their leek!"
In vain our very best haranguers,
Still by their hams reposed their hangers:

THE DINNER.

The blunderbuss still graced the hooks,
Malgrè the Constitution cooks.
Though Bentham sent the sense of ages
Boil'd down into his half-score pages;
The *weightiest* matter ever shipp'd
Since law first lodged in manuscript;
Though the fierce Colonel on them flung
Conviction in his mother-tongue."

" When from him roll'd the rights of nations,
Tropes, metaphors, hopes, adjurations;
The true-born Demosthenic thunders,
That do in Palace Yard such wonders!
And with resistless vengeance fall
Upon thy grocer Kings, Leaden Hall:
Still heads and tails alike of clans
Stuck closely to their coffee-cans.

At Monarchs when he gave his wipes,
The Capitani filled their pipes;
And, made of philosophic stuff,
Returned him gravely puff for puff!
Then asked the Embassador of Bentham
What sum in cash his Sovereign sent them?
For, though not very rapid scholars,
They have a genuine sense of dollars;
Then up the whisker'd council broke,
Ending, as it began, in smoke!"

—" A palace?"—" Yes, magnificent!
" Where every sewer bestows its scent!"
" Solid?"—" Foundation in a bog!"
" Wholesome?" " An atmosphere of fog."
" Landscape?"—" A marshy, miry flat."
" Canal?"—" A grave of dog and cat."

"Pure air?" "Where every passing puff
Is Westminster."—"Enough, enough."

—"The race—odd business; Daphne *shy!*
My Lord some thousand pounds *too* sly;
The *partners* pocketed the notes—
I'll swear three scoundrels wore their coats.
The Club examined—did their best,
And found it—honest as the rest."

Yet, spite of all their Worships' ears,
Newmarket, thou'rt the place for PEERS.
No Epsom, throng'd with city feeders—
No Doncaster, all brutes and breeders.
There Taste on all things sets her seal;
With elegance the hostlers steal;

The man that pillages your fob
But hoaxes—none would call it, rob;
The Jockey, in his speech and look,
Seems the first cousin to the Duke;
The rogue who tricks you to your face
Looks *more* than brother to his Grace;
And many a claimant of a cord
Passes for Baronet and Lord.

There, 'tis the etiquette, the winners
Ask the bedevilled to their dinners.
Oh! nights and banquets of the Gods!
What odd discussions of the odds;
What light opinions upon weights—
What cool conceptions upon heats;
What solid talk on drench and mash,
Deep things on which the wisest clash;

What lofty thoughts on hoof and heel,
Round with the brains and bottles wheel!

Claret, true Lethe of all sorrows!
Marchande of sunshines and to-morrows;
Gay doctor of all human evils—
Soft exorciser of blue devils;
Light porter of Life's heaviest loads;
Nurse of a hundred thousand odes;
Fiddle, that makes even dandies dance—
First, best embassador of France;
With more than diplomatic art,
Fixing her interests in the heart;
Lamp, that at midnight brightest glows—
Cosmetic, that tints all with rose;
Mistress, that never jilts our flame—
Beauty, for fifty years the same,

Cheerful without, as with a carriage—
Nay, even bewitching *after* marriage;
Brush, that Life's spatters out do'st rub—
Long live Queen Regent of *the* Club.

There Wh-cl-ffe counts no more his bets,
J~~ersey~~ his mortgages forgets;
Sl-g- with " both his hands in mortar,"
Scarce feels himself a shilling shorter;
The C-h-e-l,—S-ft-n,—V-r-l—,
No more take measure of a psalm;
R~~utlan~~d no more, with hair on end,
Hears all the world refuse to lend;
Nay, even the Lord of Donna Clara
Takes comfort with " *Che sarà sarà*,"
And wishes *only* hang'd the pack,
From whom no penny will come back.

THE DINNER.

How oft we've sat 'twixt sun and sun,
Nor felt the hour, my Cl-r-nd-n.
True Tories, telling every hit
That men of Fox e'er got from Pitt;
But keeping under triple locks,
What men of Pitt got back from Fox.
The B-nt-ncks, F-tzr-ys, C-v-nd-shes,
All look like—men that had their wishes;
And all is blood, bone, jest, and song,
Till morning whips the night along.

END OF CANTO II.

MAY FAIR.

CANTO III.

Gli Angeli, il Sol, la Luna erano intorno
Al Seggio di Natura in Paradiso,
Quando formaron, Signor, il vostro viso
D'ogni beltà perfettamente adorno!
Era l' aer sereno e chiaro il giorno;
Giove alternava con sua figlia il riso;
E tra le belle Grazie Amore assiso
Stavasi a mirar voi suo bel soggiorno.

FRACASTORO.

MAY FAIR.

CANTO III.

THE AFTER-DINNER.

DEDICATION.

LORD PETERSHAM.

Pleasantest of pleasant men,
Tell me in what secret den
Is your dextrous soul contriving
New dexterities in driving;
What new elegance of spur,
In the world to make a stir;

What new brilliancy of whip,
Yet to give us all the slip;
What, when ask'd at eight to dine,
Keeps you back till half-past-nine?*

---

* His Lordship is decidedly the best-bred man of the age, and abounds in pleasantries and clevernesses. But the sceptre of the *supreme bon ton* is not the lightest one in the world to carry; and etiquette is more inflexible and unintelligible than Chancery. One of its inflictions is the compelling the Noble Lord to lose his dinner. The ordinary *exquisites* come in when every one else has sat down; on the principle that the entrance of an *exquisite* ought never to be a thing unnoticed, which it might be in the crowd before. But the Monarch of the Exquisites goes beyond this; he delays his entrance until dinner is past, and then solaces himself with the fragments of the *dessert;* a proceeding which it is also etiquette to permit without the slightest obstruction.

THE AFTER-DINNER.

Forty years are gone and past—
Heavens! that years should fly so fast,—
Since the tufts vandyked your chin,
Since carmine tattooed your skin;
Since the nondescript cravat,
Since the exquisite of hat;
Boots that baffled Hoby's art,
Coat that fractured Brummel's heart;
Stays that Bartolozzi graced,
Marked you Emperor of taste.

Tell me, pleasant P———m,
Have you never felt a qualm,
When on entering the salon,
Caught your ear the parting tone;
Where the slow-retiring fair
Troop'd to coffee and despair.

Is it that you dread the spells,
Scatter'd by the man-trap belles?
Is it that your soul begins
To note the difference of skins?
You, whom young and old *chefs-d'œuvre*,
Fail'd so long to out-manœuvre.

Welcome P—t—m, at last,
Though the courses three be past;
Though the husk of peach and pine
Teach you what it *was* to dine;
Yet no soul affects surprizes—
No one at your coming rises;
Calm as if they sat at prayers,
All imbedded in their chairs:
On you not a glance is cast,
As you try to break your fast;

Every apple-rind that lingers,

Lawful capture to your fingers;

While a nut the board bestrews,

Free as air your feast to choose;

Till as closes your *dessert*,

The cross-fire talk assails your ear.

---

*" Both Houses up. A brilliant night."—

" Debate, dull, dreamy, wiredrawn, trite."—

---

* It may be a satisfaction to both parties who are now cutting each other up in the grand Council, that I am neuter, *till* the thing is decided. In my verses, I give but the clashing opinions of those who have something embarked in the battle. Like the Americans, I drive a general carrying-trade for both belligerents, and shall

"The Premier made the happiest hits."—

"The Treasury *always* has the wits."—

"The Whigs were never higher mettled."—

"Trust me, the matter's far from settled;

---

never fire a shot for either, until I see good reason why. Canning I have long observed: he is a clever, dashing eloquent fellow, as the world has not now to learn. His "Right Honourable friend on the opposite side of the house," I have long observed too; and he is a solid, strong-headed and lucky fellow. The cardinal point is, which is likely to break down first; and, until that be settled, I shall defy "my nearest and dearest friends" to discover on which side my politics lie. *Point d'argent point de Suisse* is the true language of philosophy in this delicate and high principled time. My private opinion rests in *imo pectore*, for at least a month to come.

THE AFTER-DINNER.

There's mutiny among the crew."—
" Sir, pardon me, the wine's with you.
The Whigs will have a bed of roses;"—
" True, if they count the world by noses."—
" The staunchest votes in desperate cases;"—
" Ay, just as many as get places."—
" The Earl will doubtless have the garter;"—
" His boroughs are a first-rate barter."—
" All genuine merit—your rappee."—
" Sir, many a string round many a knee
Had been much better round the neck."—
" Rely on 't, we'll not quit the deck."—
" No doubt, alone you 'll fight the guns,
When ev'ry rascal from you runs."—
" The crew will perish with the ship."—
   Rats never love their tails to dip:

The very first that smells a leak
Gives to the rest a signal-squeak;
No sooner does the light shine through,
Than ev'ry snout cries ' *Sauve qui peut,*'
Resolved in their cheese-paring souls
To die in *terra firma* holes!

No man of sense will ever swop
His conscience till he knows his shop:
The balls may shine, the cash be ready,
He'll wait to see the partners steady,
Not wishing to receive a shock
By sudden deficit of stock,
No matter whether lace or lawn
For which he put his soul in pawn.

Yet, 'tis the deuce for politicians
Wishing to better their conditions;
Accomplished men prepared to sing
Heaven save the rabble, or the King!
To live in awkward times that pose
A genius 'twixt the ayes and noes;
To keep their patriotic sense,
When England wants it! in suspense,
And see their traffic at a stop,
Until they know which *is* the shop!

If fierce on one side or on t'other,
A moment may your fortunes smother;
And yet the feeble partizan,
Whoever wins, is under ban.

'Tis pleasant to see dext'rous fools
Thus slipping 'twixt the party stools!

For me, whose multitude of sins
Is *always* friendly to the *ins;*
Whose eloquence by instinct spouts
Against those criminals the *outs*—
A patriot, Burdett to the bone,
Resolved to call my soul my own;
A loftier specimen of Brutus,
I hate to live *in medio tutus,*
Long with a pension to be tried,
And trample on the falling side.

And though (for years in Opposition)
We scorn the language of contrition;

And fifty times would rather beg,
Than to the Premier make a leg;
Yet if *he* makes the first advances,
Men should not throw away their chances:
And though *we'd* rather die than sink
To ask the thing in pen and ink;
Yet if *he* thrusts one into place,
To serve one's country 's no disgrace.

'Tis true *we* now and then abused him,
But those were trifles that amused him;
'Tis understood that ayes and noes
May differ, without being foes.
Perhaps, in some obscure debate,
Some evening when the house sat late,
We dropt, in party's usual way,
Something *we* quite forgot next day;

Some local jest, some random hit,
Some nonsense that then pass'd for wit.
But hurry, heat of argument;
Not that one likes the word,— repent,
Yet, even in party's fiercest fever,
We always thought him monstrous clever;
Though H--e might growl, and T—rn-y sneer,
The truth was neither here nor there.
Through N-wp—t's squeak, and B-xt-n's prate
We felt the leader of the State.
The idle world might call it satire,—
The world knew nothing of the matter.
But things in such a way presented
By greatness never are resented;
Mere drops between the cup and lip:
Your wisest men will sometimes trip:

In short, 'tis known, your first-rate minds
Give all offences to the winds.

We own that some *would* make a noise,—
Boys aping men—men aping boys:
But all true patriots like Jack Russell.
Though now and then they join'd the bustle;
Yet in their hearts abhorr'd the thing,
And loved, like him, the Church and King!
'Tis true, they bellow'd for Reform,
Yet, seeming hot, were scarcely warm.
Nay, all that knew their feelings best,
Knew that it made their standing jest.
Admit, they sometimes swell'd the crowd,
Their curses were not deep, though loud.
There's Gwennapp ready to make oath,
For office he was never loath;

Nay, since his tumble in the stocks,
He scorn'd the very name of Fox.
There's our great orator who wishes,
May all his bones go feed the fishes!
But, since the faction first harangued,
He wonders they escaped unhang'd.
Their muddled, mongrel, special pleadings,
Their nameless ——— House proceedings,
The nonsense that by dint of votes
They strove to cram down people's throats;
Their Constitutional infractions,
The head and tail of their transactions;
He gives them to the D——l that moved them:
They lie, that say *he* liked or loved them.
In *secret* he adored the throne;
He cares not where the secret's known.
" So your Petitioner will pray."

He farther saith, 'twas clear as day,
Six yards of ministerial silk,
At any time had changed his milk;
A black emollient for his skin,
Grown rusty with the bombasin;
But stuff eternal in and out,
The purest loyalty might rout;
Not that a treasury *could* buy him—
He wishes that they'd dare to try him,
Although at certain times a title
Might seem to some a fit requital,—
Not that he meant to eat his words,
To be a lord,—or fifty lords.

" The vessel gone ?"—" High hopes of Parry,"*

" Sure as my grandam to miscarry;"

" He takes five hundred pecks of coals !"

" No doubt he 'll liquify the poles;"

---

* P—y is a shrewd, enterprizing, and frost-defying personage as any in his Majesty's dominions; no man alive can object to him for doing his best to get a ship; nor for making an expedition once a-year; nor for making a book out of that expedition; nor for having attempted impossibilities and failed; nor for having done nothing where nothing was to be done. If the philosophers of Somerset House, and the ship-people of that *ci-devant* Scotch Palace, near the Horse Guards, had recommended a voyage to the Moon, Captain P—— would have been right in offering himself for inspection, ready with three months' provisions in his haversack, wings at his back, the new patent air-generator in his pocket, to resist the rarefaction

"He's ballasted with flying sledges."

" The saints preserve the Arctic hedges!

" Some gallons of Sir Humphrey's acid,"

" Just half a pint makes ocean placid ;"

---

of the upper regions, and a map of the course by Bishop Wilkins in his better hand. But the grand affair rests with the advisers, promoters, and *profiters*—the *onus* must be borne by those who felt so enamoured of territory, that they looked for it twenty degrees beyond the possible climates of life ; and the more they failed the more they looked. And all this in the teeth of all experience, in the outcry of every man who had been in the Arctic Seas, and in scorn of all science. The true expedition must be by land, and this was told to the ship-people from the beginning. Little fat Franklin would have ascertained in a week more than all that could have been settled by all the years of ship-freezing and pantomime-playing since

" A liquid, with a Bramah stopper,

For raising"—" Brushwood upon copper."

" A set of patent music-boxes

To lure the buffaloes and foxes;

French watches for the Polar frows,

The new steam-acting Perkins' ploughs;

The seeds of all the favourite spices,

The last machines for making ices.—

The cargo quite a thing of tact."

—" Sir! listen, if you like a fact:

---

the flood. The Captain is now gone to try his fortune in another style; and if he will find out for us of what the Pole is made, or whether there is any Pole at all, a matter long doubted in the Pump-room at Bath, and at present forming the chief conversation of that accomplished city, we shall be at last obliged to him.

THE AFTER-DINNER.

After three months' ice-parading,
After three months' masquerading,
After three months' knocks and bumps
That bring his lugger to her stumps;
After loss of pipes and spoons,
Deficit of pantaloons;
Hairbreadth scapes of white bear paws,
Sentimental loves of squaws;
Just as he espied the channel,
Brought to his last yard of flannel;
All his best cigars burnt out,
Winds all whistling "right about;"
Quarter-day you'll have him back,
With his volume in his pack."

Out the wonder comes at last
Wondering how it came so fast—

All the world, including M-rr-y,
In a philosophic flurry;
All the botanizing belles,
All whom Brande provides with smells,
Priest of all the chemic loves,
Lovely in his kidskin gloves;
All the twaddlers of the Alfred,
All the quarter and the half-read;
All the paper-headed members
Shivering over learning's embers;
All Parnassus' wither'd shrubs,
All the sages of the Clubs;
All the doldrum F R. S.'s,
Deep in duckweed, straws, and cresses;
Worthy measurers of dust—
Worthy of Sir Joseph's bust,

Worthy to complete the ranks
Of the mighty name of B-nk-s,
Deep in nondescript descriptions,
Puzzling as their own Egyptians;
All the wiseacres on filberts,
All the world of D—s G-lb-rts;
All the guilty candle-burners,
F-tt-ns, Sabines, D-ws-n T——s;
Lecturers on a gnat's proboscis,
Oracles in mire and mosses;
Hunters up of Autographs—
At whose labours mankind laughs;
Delving through the hideous scribbles
Of forgotten knaves and fribbles.

All thy tribe, Lord Aberdeen,
Sense and nonsense stuck between;

Wise in all things dead and rotten,
Useful as a herring shotten;
Solemn beggars, in whose bags
All the gathering is rags.
Learning's resurrection-men,
Wielders of the church-yard pen,
Worthy of the plundered lead—
Worms, that feed but on the dead:
Sweeps, that never lift their eyes
Where the flames of Learning rise;
But beside its altar's foot
Fill their pouches with the soot.
All the crazing, and the crazed,
Hurry all—to be amazed!

Page by page unrolls before ye
Britain's Argonautic glory;

THE AFTER-DINNER.

How the grand Discovery Fleet,

Several months sail'd several feet.—

" Sunday, hanging o'er the stove,

Thought the vessel *meant* to move.

Monday, rather felt the frost;

Tuesday, thump'd, and crost, and tost;

Wednesday, kick'd from post to pillar,

Knock'd the nozzle off the tiller;

Thursday, white bears in the distance,

Kill'd, long shots, severe resistance;

Ate a sailor once or twice—

White bears seldom over nice.

Friday, Mercury at zero,

Every soul on board a hero.

Saturday, all cased in rime,

Scarcely thaw'd at pudding-time;

Every nose of land or able,

Living ices at the table;

Crystallizing in a row,

Fine as Jarrin's* Christmas show.

But the keenest was to come:

Muse of History be dumb!

Though the passage lay in sight,

Somewhere to the left or right;

---

* I have, I pledge myself as a public man and a patriot, examined every system that has done honour to the noble Science of Gastronomy, and as a matter of equal justice and gratification I must give my opinion in favour of Jarrin, in the whole department of Marmalade, &c. His book I keep upon my pillow, as Alexander kept the Iliad for his midnight inspiration. Ude I *know*, a more matchless man. ·r of the *cuisine* was never under noble roof; popularity followed his soups; and his volume is the supreme ornament of my library.—(S—n.)

Or behind them, or before them,
Home the scoundrel breezes bore them.
But next summer 'twill be found,
Who will bet ten thousand pound?

But there's something for the *blues,*
Grieving for their two pound twos.
Not a squaw but has a story,
Not a flea but skips before ye.
You've a list of every needle,
That could soul or body wheedle.
Tare and tret of every quid,
That for dog or duckling bid:
How much brandy in her water,
Warm'd old Sealskin's oily daughter.
Every bill on Monmouth-street,
Paid for leagues of genuine sleet:

Every Admiralty name,
Yet to fill the trump of fame :
All the mighty officemen,
Perch'd on stock, and rock, and fen;
Puzzling all the blubber hordes,
With Lords—alas! no longer Lords.
There (every dog will have his day,)*
Bold C-b-n towers through fog and spray;

---

* This distribution of territory was first conceived, to do him justice, by Captain Ross; who, to do him justice again, was a very smart, ingenious, and *injured* officer. But it may be fairly questioned, and will no doubt become a subject of national remonstrance in the earliest Esquimaux Parliament, particularly if the Polar circle should be so far advanced in civilization as to be looking round the world for some nation to pelt with snowballs.—" What right," will the Esquimaux Ambassador say, " can a British

H-pe boasts a marsh, and gallant M-re
Is monarch of a mile of shore:
Ill-omen'd Melville has his isle,
Grim as his own paternal pile;
Where the great scion of D-nd-s
May graze his goose, and ride his ass:

---

marauder have to distribute the titles of the Arctic Empire? or what right can he have to inflict upon it the obscure appellations of the officials of a power forty degrees South of the only climate where man is to be found in his original dignity, the land flowing with oil, clothed in ermine, lighted by the glitter of the Aurora; and by a sunshine that throws the decrepit day of the South into contempt; not of twelve hours, but of four thousand!" Let the Admiralty look to it, and abolish their usurpations in good time.

Nay, not a messenger or clerk,
But in some mire has made his mark,
And stamp'd by *friendship's* broadest arrow,
Looms through eternal mists Cape B-rr-w.

" B—— caught at last?"—"Yes, limed for life,
Condemn'd to virtue and a wife."
" Too happy dog! he now relaxes
His purse-strings but to pay his taxes:
A gentle hermit in his cell,
He pokes the fire, and pulls the bell;

---

* The actual ceremony has been made an affair of some scepticism among a particular set; and undoubtedly, for the present, like American news, or like the new Ministry, or as the Rogers (always inimitable) adds, "like the little girls in St. James's Parish, it wants *confirmation.*"

Upon his knee his babies dandles,

Concocts the tea, and snuffs the candles;

Scarce in the mirror gives a glance,

Lets even his ringlets take their chance;

Cares not a farthing if the Craven

Was lost by jockeyship or spavin;

If, at the paying of the stakes,

The doer or the done was R——;

In fact, has turn'd a new Hughes Ball,

A rustic pattern to *us* all."

" *Sweet Mercandetti, if such ladies

Could often be invoiced from Cadiz,—

---

* The prettiest importation that we have had since the war. Nothing is more remarkable than the extraordinary

Such raven locks, such sparkling eyes,
Were voted in the home supplies;
Such fairy feet, such taper fingers—
They'd make the fortune of the bringers:
Even I, who dread the name of wife,
Might order—per the good ship, F——.

---

ill-luck or infirm taste of the whole tribe of our military, naval, civil, and exploratory persons on the Continent, in the matter of wives. They seem to have been acted on by a curious felicity in the selection of ugliness; and there is no doubt that we have returned the compliment very effectually in the helpmates with which we have punished the whiskered lovers of English guineas. The traffic in the live-stock is the counterpart of the traffic in the dead. The Englishman sends abroad his faded manufactures, and gets rid of them at any price. The Continental returns them with varnished pictures, mutilated statues, cracked vases, and mummies.

THE AFTER-DINNER.

'Tis pleasant, in this world of fools,
To look on Nature's finer tools,
To see the light of jetty eyes
Take Bond-street heroes by surprise;
Till the white-heat of beauty's fire
Melts down the dandy to the squire.
'Tis pleasant, when, like mother Eve's,
Spring makes her petticoat of leaves,
To see him run the homely round
Of husbands fairly in the pound.
How lightly in thy ear-drums B-ll*
The names of R-s and Lenox fall!

---

* This gentleman's taste in cabs and cravats first distinguished him. For a time he was remarkably in flower and narrowly escaped being at once the *beau* of the season, a legislator for seven years, and a Benedick for life, or

Not caring for the world a button,
You brew your beer, and kill your mutton;
At morn, *costumed* in fustian breeches,
You watch your architects of ditches;
Receive returns of hens and cocks,
Put corn and duck eggs under locks;

---

the caprice of the most captivating and capricious of high-born enslavers: but destiny is irresistible, and it was his destiny to be pierced by the blackest pair of eyes within the memory of man; to have become a scorner of supremacy in the cravat system; and to have finally subsided into the most hospitable of country gentlemen. His claret is first-rate; his preserve is excellent; and his *menage* is superintended by the most select professor of the culinary science on this side of Paris. If he sets up for the county, he shall have my plumper. (Punt. J——.)

Look sharply to those rogues the grooms,
Embezzlers of your mops and brooms,
Prove that your talent 's not mistaken
In matters relative to bacon ;
Trim up the pheasant-stealing sinner,
And come exact at five to dinner.

Then take your evening wine and sitting,
Inspector of Senora's knitting ;
Or order out your country cab,
Give whip and rein to your Queen Mab ;
(And scarcely in a poet's dream,
A prettier hand e'er touch'd her team ;)
And take the wisdom of the village
On last year's frost, and next year's tillage.

Hear men, Heaven knows who made their co
Discuss the latest price of oats;
And drop your summons with the vicar,
To give his verdict on your liquor.

Until the sunshine's rosy dip,
Faint rival of your lady's lip;
And the breeze across the hill,
Warns you that you're standing still,
And a glance towards your oaks
Shows your curling household smokes,
Shows you that your lamps are lighted,
Shows, if you stop, you'll be benighted.

Too happy fellow, in those glances
You're safe from Fortune's tricksy chances:

Though O-tl-nds to the hammer fall,
You have two diamonds worth it all;
Nay, should your final shilling vanish,
The R—rs vows " you 'll have the *Spanish*."

Oh clouds! ye wandering wayward things,
Substantial nothings, waveless wings;
Ye thrones of hyacinth and rose,
Where spirits in their flight repose;
Ye pearl and purple vales of bliss,
Ye islands of the blue abyss,
Ye steeds,—whom every laurell'd bard,
Has since the deluge rode so hard;
Making, of your manes and tails,
Similes for maids and males.
Every soul has had a time
When he thought himself sublime,

When he dream'd his hour was come,
When he must no more be dumb;
Mounted in Apollo's boots,
Well supplied with moonlight lutes;
Piled with Venice-hat and feathers,
When he should defy all weathers;
With his music of the spheres,
Taking mankind by the ears.

Dan Apollo! fool-enslaver,
When I had your worship's fever,
(But a sort of schoolboy tertian,
Cured by Newmarket immersion,)
I have stood at set of sun,
Cloud-collecting, one by one;
Wild with all their twistings, turnings,
Softenings, sweetenings, fadings, burnings;

Building in each ruddy stain,
Glorious " *Chateaux en Espagne;*"
Watching the delicious twilight
Peeping from her Eastern skylight;
Like an Andalusian maid
Listening to a serenade:
Like a vestal freshly sainted,
With her cheek half pale, half painted;
Like a Turkish beauty showing
Through her veil the roses glowing;
Till, 'twas but a softer morn,
Silvery rose the Lunar horn.

Or around her high abode,
Tempest, like an ocean, flow d;
Till the lightning's sulphur-gleam
Flamed on mountain, vale, and stream;

And the vaporous upper world
Roll'd, like armies downward hurl'd,
Titans, by the thunder driven
From the sapphire gates of Heaven;
While the swellings of the gale
Seem'd their trumpet's broken wail.
Then along the mighty blue
Rose like flowerets pale and few,
Over which a storm had gone,
Star and starlet, one by one;
Like the lamps in some high fane,
Struggling through the tempest-stain;
As it vanish'd, richer mustering,
Orb on orb in glory clustering;
Till the temple of the night
Blazed with the immortal light.

Trifles—fancy's long past gleams,—
Boyish, more than boyish dreams;
Things of many a year ago—
Yet what have our years to show,
With their thousand secret stings,
Better than those boyish things?
From our cradles to our shrouds,
What are hopes, joys, loves,—but clouds?

END OF CANTO III.

MAY FAIR.

CANTO IV.

Dangle.—I'faith I would not have told—but it's in the papers, and your name at full length in the Morning Chronicle.

Puff.—Ah! those damn'd editors never can keep a secret.

Sheridan's Critic.

MAY FAIR.

CANTO IV.

THE MIDNIGHT DRIVE.

DEDICATION.

TO ———

* Sweet ———, by that host of spells
That break the hearts of all our belles;

---

* Though I never intentionally look into a newspaper, yet by accident I have observed the name of a lady of rank annexed to this my fourth Canto. Am I to apologize or atone for this? or is not the apology to be looked

By those two lips, a rosy wreath
Around those more than pearly teeth;
By those two eyes of living light;
I swear to live thy faithful knight.

Though all the girls that feed on Greek;
Though all the girls that tint a cheek;

---

for in the utter impossibility of doing anything so idle as making common fame my *confidante* on the occasion. To that lady, however, whom to name is to panegyrise, I desire to make my most anxious acknowledgments; and to assure her that, be the object of my lines what they may, she would deserve a much better bard, though she could not find a more devoted one: but after all, she is not *the* lady, the fair and fantastic idol, on whose *toilette* I now offer up those lines, to be turned into *papillotes*, if such be her sovereign pleasure.

Though all the girls from sixty downwards,
That force their gouty fathers townwards;
Though all the girls whom coronets
Keep practising in morning sets;
Though all the girls of mathematics;
Though all the Amazons or Attics;
Though all the lovely premature,
Devote themselves to work my cure;—
Yet, till the hour I make my will,
Thou, thou shalt be my empress still.

Three Cantos, like Canova's Graces,*
Three charmers with three sister-faces,

---

* All the world have, of course, admired Canova's Graces; whose chief merit is, however, that they are like three pretty English school-girls. Italy has certainly no-

Free, fond, and frolic as the wind,
By this time have the world entwined :
Now, o'er my loveliest and my last
The lustre of thy smile be cast ;
With Beauty's Sovereign on my side,
I wish the world were twice as wide.

Idol, that might'st have sat or stood
For Venus rising from the flood ;

---

thing to do with them. They want the *tragique* look that belongs to the higher order of the Italian models. They are happily destitute of that eager affectation, that makes every pretty Frenchwoman on earth look as if she had just escaped from the *coulisses* of the Opera Comique. Their innocence, sweetness, and touching simplicity, are English, and English alone:—the artist must have dreamed them.

Fresh sparkling from the morning dip,
Ere breeze of earth profaned her lip;
Ere touched her ivory foot the ground,
Ere felt her bosom woe or wound,
Ere from her locks had dropt a pearl,
The model of a " taking girl"—
The prettiest pattern of coquette,
That ever made man foolish yet:
The sweetest sinner of fifteen,
That ever play'd coquette or queen.

*'Tis evening, June in all its might,
Broad day,—at ten o'clock at night.

---

* One of the most formidable inconveniences of our inconvenient climate. The poets, a race of observers of

Tired of my lord's tenth, tenth told story,
Forgetting that the day's before ye:—

Nature, who yet see less of her than any other race of mankind, with perhaps the exception of a Cornish miser, or that most imprisoned of prisoners, and most miserable of men, a Lord Chancellor,—talk perpetually of the charms of an English twilight: they might talk as rationally of the charms of a consumption; the slow decay of day; the dreary appearance of every thing visible; the chill, clayey, colourless clouds that absolutely look tired of lingering hour after hour; and the brown blaze that *will* keep disfiguring the dinner-table, that excludes the chandeliers, and utterly destroys the effect of rouge, dress, and diamonds.

Those things are "ordered better" in the South: the sun there keeps as regular hours as a gouty gentleman; rises as if his physician prescribed six o'clock, and goes to bed not a minute after his time. Those who have driven

THE MIDNIGHT DRIVE. 147

Expecting to find earth in gloom,
You sally from the heated room,
And find, no matter where you drive,
The world with vulgars all alive.

Ye well-bred charms of southern skies,
Where daylight by appointment dies;
Where, just as your Siesta's done,
Dead to a second drops the sun:
As dead as ever melo-drame,
Engender'd 'twixt K-n-r-d and L-m-b;
As dead as Antipope professions
Of Mister B-nk-s's final sessions.

---

through the Alameda of any Spanish town after dusk or have sallied out into the Toledo, will know the charm of the contrast—it is a *charm*, and indescribable.

'Tis sweet Italian Night; you rise,
The rabble vanish from your eyes:
Ten thousand figures round you flit,
They 're seen as much as H-rt-n's wit.
You hear a whisper, smell cigars,
Catch the low twanging of guitars;
And, but where Punch sets up his camp,
Or where " Our Lady" lights her lamp,
While some sweet face beneath it twinkles,
Fresh from its holy water sprinkles;
Or lights and chanting in some chapel,
Remind you that you 're still " *en Naples;*"
You 'd think the locomotive hosts
Were very easy manner'd ghosts.

While *here*, the night will never drop,
Go where you will, you meet the shop.

Whirl to the West, you find the park
But turn'd a fuller Noah's ark;—
Whirl to the North, the favourite spot
For *us* to breakfast and be shot;
The feed and fight alike are o'er,
  * Chalk Farm is now Chalk Farm no more.

---

* Chalk Farm, once the chosen theatre of well-bred *exits*. But the shade of honour has been driven from the place by the barbaric invasion of brick! The unfortunate landlord, who used to calculate on the results of an angry parliamentary session—the bitterness of the exiled—or the lie direct from the winning-side, with the regularity of an Insurance office, must be in a state of hopeless exasperation. Fashion might as well settle her affairs in the centre of Fleet-street. Language, too, will lose a valued part of its phraseology; we shall never again hear a Bond-street belligerent characterized as a "Chalk-Farm subject." R-g-rs,

There, Nash, thy plaster town aspires,—
Retreat of Moorfields and Black Friars.
The stucco fine, the gravel finer;
The lamps divine, the lake diviner.—

---

to whom I acknowledge my verses indebted for all their *lustre*, recommends that the landlord should, in memory of the departed weapon, hang up for his sign " Ancient Pistol!" " Heu quanto minus est cum aliis," &c. As to what has usurped the classic ground, I can say but little from personal observation. It is rather distant from the world; but I suppose a number of very respectable persons have wound up their city matters to club there, and that it may be a sufficiently pleasant retreat from selling ribbons, &c. Crockford's having posted himself there is of itself symptomatic of something to be got; and possibly in a generation or two he may put some of them in circumstances not to be easily distinguished from those of persons of the first fashion in Town.

THE MIDNIGHT DRIVE.

The whole affair superbly pretty!
The whole,—the trader and his city.
There pant, uneasy for their life,
Fat pair, the alderman and wife;
There groans the Genius of some ward,
For twelve revolving months, my Lord!
The bulky owner of Molasses
Envies his happier brother asses:
The *worthy*, rich from porcine slaughter,
Curses the day he saw its water;
All round the wretch so ultra fine—
*He dreads to stir, sit, sleep, or dine.

---

* The Marquis, (soon to be no Marquis,) the leader of every thing *comme il faut*, and giver of the most accomplished dinners on this side of the Equator, has settled

Yet there, if men their eyes will ope,
They'll find *en costume à la Hope,*

---

down in the Regent's Park: it was an absolute mercy;— not that the place is to be laughed at as a specimen of the skill of our modern architects, for all the *façades* are showy, and some are fine and Palladian; but it has had the misfortune to be delivered over to all the absurdities of an opulent populace, the very *pis aller* of speculation, all things that no one would suffer any where else, make their experiments there. There stood the Ophthalmic Hospital, which one could not approach within a mile without the chance of paying an eye as the price of the adventure. There explodes the new patent gun, that is to shake the towers of Cronstadt or Constantinople, of which my Lord Marquis carries a pattern in his pocket, along with the Garter, as an alternative for the Emperor Nicholas. There winds the Canal to receive all the Thames coal-barges, and love-stricken waiting-maids! There the London and Edinburgh New-Philosophy-Politi-

Temptation fresh from London Wall,
The beauty of the Easter ball;

---

cal-Reform-College-Committee, have actually laid hold of a district for some of their nameless purposes; and there, though the lesser evil, the Zoological Society have designed a new Seminary for tigers, leopards, lions, and similar ornamental, useful, and safe assistants to civilization and the nineteenth century: the whole to be disposed strictly according to their *habitats*. Jungles are already in great forwardness; the boa-constrictor has already expressed his satisfaction at the swamp which has been so ingeniously provided for him: and the cobra de capellos, tiger-cats, and panthers, will feel perfectly at home.— Doubtless, for a while, a few nursery-maids and children in arms will occasionally be missed. A contemplative gentleman taking his evening-walk, may be surprised into a very unexpected study of Natural History; and an inquest may be held on even an alderman found in the

From three months finishing in France
Return'd, with Death in every glance;
A half De Stael, half Eloise,
To trample the piano's keys—
To blot black beetles upon paper—
To light the " Muse's midnight taper;"
To sigh for " dear Count Strogonoff,"
(A valet that nigh whisk'd her off;)
To dream of " Marquis Romanzini,"
(You'd buy the scoundrel for a guinea;)
To heave the breast, and roll the eye,
And lisp, " Di tanti palpiti!"

---

custody of the " Forest King." But those necessary *accidents* will diminish as the Regent's Park becomes more exclusively devoted to Zoological science: when none but Professors invade its precincts, of course none but professors will be eaten.

Yet, in those cit-infested valleys,
Before for polar frost he sallies,
To drive in Tartar skulls the sense
Of " Honi soit qui mal y pense ;"
As no man's fitter for this barter,
Than he who once has " caught a Tartar ;"
Gay Hertford rears his Tuscan dome,
For lordly fashion's lordliest home.

Land of the North, enchanting clime,
Where Summer sits enthron'd in slime!
Where Winter, quick as winds can blow,
O'erlays the aforesaid slime with snow ;
And fog, and frost, and mire together,
No doubt make very pleasant weather ;
Ten years are gone (my tears flow fast !)
Since on your charms I gazed my last—

Since in all jargons under heaven
My vows were to your charmers given;
To swampy Holland's maids of mud—
To Denmark's, fish in face and blood;
To greasy Teutchland's thick-legged vro
To Sweden's, kindred to their cows;
To all diversities of skin,
Through Peter's realms of oil and gin;
Where lovers overhead in love
Make speeches bottom'd on a stove;
And maidens touch'd with mutual flame,
Return them,—bottom'd on the same.
H-tf-d, beware of tender passions,
Until you know the Calmuck fashions;
The man caught serenading there,
Will soon betray a *loss of car*.

Or, if unsnipt the stanza flows,
The zephyr mulcts you in a nose;
There Cupid has no time to linger,
Each moment costs a toe or finger;
You 're lucky if you quit the place
The half-possessor of your face.
The maiden that is over nice
Will see her love *preserved* in ice.
Transcendent soil of fen and fog,
Where man is but a larger frog!

* The Haymarket 's a burst of light;
The Opera—mighty Pasta's night!

---

* Pasta, a very powerful performer: since Catalani, the Italian stage has produced no more brilliant and com-

Bold, splendid, tragic, first the song
Bursts like a cataract along;
Then, like a mountain stream subsiding,
Between its banks of roses gliding,
The harmony, sweet, solemn, clear,
In new enchantment bathes the ear.
Yet noble as her noblest strain,
The *actress* o'er us throws the chain;
The queenly step, the depth of eye,
The strife of passion wild and high,
The art, true nature's matchless art,
Its strength, its burning source, the heart;

---

manding voice. Her acting is still rarer upon the stage; and those who have not seen her Medea and Semiramide have yet to learn the power of combined gesture and song.

THE MIDNIGHT DRIVE. 159

The searching *agony* of tone,
Make all the struggling soul her own.

The spell dissolved,—I take my rounds ;
A licensed sportsman on those grounds :
The rich preserve, that few approach,
Without a title and a coach ;
But *I*, who " know the price of stocks,"
Cry " Sesame !" to every box ;
They know *I* scorn the charming ties,
So take my folly as it flies.
We settle " who escapes to Paris,"—
" Whose in the Austrian box the star is ;
" What *wonder* in the red and yellow
" Has fix'd thy *lorgnette,* Count Palmella ;
" What whisker'd monster, Mynheer Falck!
" Holds in such *very* solemn talk ;

" Whose cheeks and chin are *too* much *tinted*,
" Whose marriage has been *more* than hinted;
" Whom all-resistless Polignac
" Has kept this fortnight on the rack;
" Whom Lieven thinks the Belle to-night,
" (The Prince is always in the right);
" For whom is built the Viscount's villa,—
" But hark,—'tis magic, or Brambilla."

Then drops the eye upon the pit,
Where dandies stand, and dowdies sit;
The irksome prison of he-brutes.
That to their beds would take their boots;
Where St-nh-pe in the foremost tier,
Performs an extra chandelier,
Reflecting on his polish'd forehead
The light from every stage-lamp borrow'd.

* Or, where the Foreign Office nest

Shews fifty in a box comprest;

The diplomatic exquisites!

Copies of statesmen, beaux, and wits.

Thus men, ordain'd the world to master

Give their fac-similes in plaster;

---

* Downing-street has its representative majesty in the Opera House, in the shape of a whole desk-full, I beg pardon, box full of very well-dressed young gentlemen. They attend with great decorum to the performance, carry on their diplomatic etiquette to each other with great gravity, and, unless when the shoe of a *figurante* flies into their box, from its peculiar proximity to the stage, or the kettle-drums are engaged in a charge, seem to be happy. Yet it is painful to see them so dismally squeezed together; though it must be allowed that they suffer with the patience of martyrs.

And Chathams, Wellingtons, and Naps,
Are sold by Savoyards for raps.

" The Colonel? yes, he never misses,
Since F-fe deserted the coulisses.
Why sits he from the crowd aloof,
Gazing so fiercely on the roof?"
" 'Tis whisper'd that he comes to town
Express, to have the house knock'd down."

* Yet I like thee, pleasant Trench;
Though the sages of the Bench

---

* The Irish Colonel, one of the pleasantest persons possible at one's table, yet a confoundedly awkward person to let into one's house. His first conception is always, how much it would be improved by being burned, or blown up, or beaten down, or in some way or other scattered into thin air, and swept from the face of earth. Of course,

Would not give a single stiver

For thy bridge *along* the river:

---

this is in no hostility to you; for no man has more of the good-nature of his country about him; but the public good must be paramount. He has an improving spirit, a subversive soul: the besom of destruction is the sceptre of his ambition, as Sheridan said of the French Revolutionists; he rejoices "in the wreck of matter, and the crush" of houses.

Si fractus illabatur orbis,
Impavidum ferient ruinæ.

There can be no doubt that he has several plans in his portfolio for the new World; and that he would be charmed by the first symptoms that the old one was going into cinders.

Yet the Colonel has taste: some of his designs are extremely happy; and far be it from any man who desires to see fortune, intelligence, and place in society, occupied in

Though the dames of Billingsgate
Swore to duck thee soon or late;
Though the guardians of the mud
Would have swamp'd thee, ebb or flood;

---

manly and graceful pursuits, to find fault with his occupation. At the same time, I should recommend it to any gentleman who wishes to keep his house over his head, to keep the Colonel's eyes off it if he can. He will otherwise unquestionably find it pointed out in the next plan of some new Square, or Street, or Circus, or Abattoir, as a thing utterly incompatible with the well-being of his Majesty's good City of London. Apsley House had a narrow escape not long since: but report says, that a company of the First Guards were brought up, with orders to fire on the first man who approached the house with any symptoms of a surveyor about him. It has stood, and the great Duke has not thus to lament at once the loss of his place and his local habitation: but let minor men beware!

Though the grisly men of coals
Rose in black fan-hatted shoals;
Though the sapient aldermen
Fought thee with ill-spelling pen;
Though the doubly sapient Mayor
Thunder'd nonsense from *the* chair;
Though against thee spouted Cam,
(Wolf that crush'd the bleat of L-mb;)
Sings *the* Rogers—" Classic streams,
Long may the Cam defend the Thames!"
* Though Whig—Tory—Neuter Jack
Threw his burden on thy back;

---

* As a politician Lord John has his principles still to settle; and perhaps no man has a right to blame him much, at a time when Whig and Tory are so pleasantly flung into conjunction, when even the " dii majorum

•Though the man of the Bazaar
On thee turn'd his stable war,

---

gentium," the fiercest champions, the men who had sworn by all the darker divinities, are turned into such happy and harmless lovers of things as they are, that even Sir Frank, "for his part, knows no difference between Whig and Tory!" and even says this, without any visible consciousness of its effect on the muscles of mankind. But Lord J., removed from his puzzled politics, has qualities that, if clouded, cannot be extinguished by party. He is a poet, a scholar, and when he speaks uncrushed by the consciousness of the unnatural union between the son of nobility and the very refuse of the Radical mire, he is a very interesting speaker.

* Mab—a genius for all things, carriage, cab, fish, finance, bank, brick-making, and for that species of eloquence which Sir Joseph Yorke, in his characteristic way, calls general botheration. Waithman's appearance in the House has disturbed his supremacy in news fresh from the City,

Libel, paragraph, and plate,
Showering round thy patriot pate;
Pealing vengeance in thy ear
The whole *grande nation boutiquière*.

I own, I like this easy talking,
A kind of Opera sleep-walking;
Just made for lazy brains like mine!
Let wits and sages strive to shine,
My loveliest of all lovely things
Is woman, angel without wings;
Yet if there's horror beyond human,
To me 'tis *philosophic* woman.

---

with which it was his privilege to delight those of less extensive adventure eastward; and in revenge he has lately set up a haberdasher's shop on a scale large enough to drive the Alderman to despair.

Although you ate your primal steaks
Among the honest Oxford Greeks,
Or suck'd your dose of British port
Where Euclid holds by Cam his Court;
Or in Ierne's "Silent Sister"
*Spunged on the vintner and the *pistor*.

---

* The Dublin University has the honour of being called the Silent Sister throughout Europe; and she has, what is rare in this world of misapplied names, the merit of fully deserving the appellation. Yet the Irish in general are the very antipodes of either indolence or stupidity. The Burkes, Sheridans, Currans, and so forth, would be pledges for the capabilities of a people more proverbially Bœotian than our pleasant brothers beyond the Channel. But the truth is, that the system of the University is utterly ineffectual in all its shapes, as an exciter and instructor of the national ability. Genius is smothered in mathematics. By an anomaly altogether inconceivable, the great ab-

Ierne! theme of many a line,
That never trickled from the Nine;

---

sorbing distinction, the trumpet of fame in the Irish University, is an aptness for Algebra. What is the result? In a nation remarkable for a vividness of conception, which we may detect in the common language of the people; for a turn of mind which may almost be called classic; for a spirit, ardour, and ease of language, which make the natural materials of the great orator, writer, and philosopher; we have nothing but some miserable schoolboy expertness in the rule of three. That there are able intellects to be found among the professors and students, none can doubt; but what *student* does the Irish University send out armed for the great contests of public life? What contribution does its whole body make to even the cause of its struggling and brow-beaten Religion on the spot! Still less what work of classical scholarship, or public importance, has it added to the general literature of England! or still less, to the permanent literature of Eu-

Ierne, land of bulls and cows,
Of many an English widow's spouse,
Of proud and patriot absentees,
Of rich reversionary fees,
Of old rebellion's glowing embers!
Of just one hundred virtuous Members,

---

rope! Nay, even in the narrow, puzzled, and impotent circle of its own ambition, what has it produced? what *discoveries* has it made? how many *mathematicians* has it sent into the world within the *last hundred years?*

The Irishmen of ability whom we occasionally meet with in London, are no contradiction to this. They have received their "second education" in general English life; and have been suffered to follow the natural direction of their minds. Among no class of men are to be found more strenuous deplorers of the disastrous, purblind, and totally unnational bias of the system of their University.

As sapient as the dames that bore them,
As modest as their sires before them;
All dumb—of which I'm no regretter,
(The less that's sometimes said the better.)
Yet, when a good thing's in the wind,
No man will think them deaf or blind;
Not but I know they hate a job,
Though such *might* fill a patriot's fob;
Not but I know, in all their garrets
They'd scorn to act the treasury parrots;
Or crowd upon a *special* night,
To stand the drill " eyes left or right,"
Or make the *rather* thicker calls,
In Whitehall when a peerage falls:
Yet no twelve men on earth would find
Those patriots either deaf or blind!

Ierne, true Romance's spot,

Alike by Heaven and Earth forgot!

Thy people gayest of the gay,

Where every ribbon breeds a fray!

Thy soil the richest of the rich,

Where famine huts in every ditch!

Holy dominion of the Pope!

Ruled by the musket and the rope!

Pure gem of the Atlantic flood,

With every field, a field of blood!

*Yet, seated by an Edinbro' dame

Away at once goes all your fame:

---

* I remember at the Caledonian ball in Edinburgh, to have been entrapped, by the pastoral look of a very

In vain you 've woo'd the classic muse,

You 're nothing in the land of trews;

In vain before your Oxford quorum

You 've worked the Typ: Barytonorum,

Or all your cerebellum puzzled

To find in logic reason muzzled,

While Davison the disputatious

Made all your syllogisms fugacious;

---

pretty girl, into asking her hand for the next dance. In the interval I tried to ascertain how far she had been imbued with the love of roses and lilies, of blue floods and romantic hills. My pretty partner looked at me with utter contempt! and returned my lucubrations by a very *recherché* character of Mr. Maculloch's Political Economics, with an Episode on the Government of India.

In vain Darii and Bocardo,
Unless you 've thumb'd our friend Ricardo;
Your Wisdom's in a genuine stew,
Unless you 've read the last Review.
What know you of the safety-valve?
How schistus splits, or camels calve?
How modern population thickens?
How stoves increase the breed of chickens
How nature in her human sluices
Makes gastric and th' et cetera juices?
How every blue-bell has its spouse,
True to its vegetable vows?
How hornstein, trap, and selenite,
Were made before earth saw the light?
How true philosophy exposes
The terrible mistakes of Moses?—

How cows communicate their thoughts?
How all the lights of Earth are Scots?

But hush?—the *Déesse* of the ballet,
The woe and wonder of Fop's-alley,
Where T——re in ecstasies
Forgets the fire of *Spanish* eyes.
She comes!—Soft, sparkling, like a star,
Floats on her sylphid wing, Brocard:
Beside the beauty, gay Fleurot
Floats, witchery from top to toe.
I glance a moment, feel my heart
Not meant to act a Roman part;
Make my best bow to all the fair,
And whirl full gallop to *the* square.

Along the streets the chamber-light,
Shows toilets busy for the night.

Oh! for a touch of friend Asmodeus,
A station on some roof commodious;
To watch, without a compound fracture,
The sweet, man-killing manufacture!—
There beauty in her mirror grows,
Let rivals hate the shape it shows.
Now wreathe the brow the raven tresses,
A smile the dear effect confesses:
Now round the neck the diamonds glitter
No cynic could at this look bitter.
On goes the jewel-bound panache;
Her eyes return it flash for flash.
The tissued silk, the Brussels lace,
What wonder if she like *that* face?—
'Tis but plain justice to admire
That shape, that step, that eye of fire.

Last, o'er her shoulders drops the shawl,
To hide, in mercy to us all,
What,—if I dar'd to speak my mind,
Might make, but never meet, me blind.

There stands a figure for thee, Lawrence,
Worth all the belles of Rome or Florence:
Thou, whose immortalizing touch,
Defies old Time's hard-handed clutch;—
Gives light to eyes, and bloom to lips,
That scorn a century's eclipse,
That even when L-c-s-t-r's self is past,
Her charms shall round our grandsons cast.—
On Hope's fair brow bid beauty sit,
Flash life from Jersey's eye of wit;

MAY FAIR.

And show how majesty can fling
Its mantle o'er a patriot KING.

Young ladies all, pray take example
From this, (by no means single sample,)
Of how much pleasanter 'tis dressing,
To constitute a ball-room's blessing;
Taking from every curl the papers,
In sight of half a dozen tapers;
Giving your beauty between whiles
Those sweet anticipation smiles,
By which the bosoms of five hundred,
Ere morn, shall of their hearts be plunder'd,—
Than sitting up without a light,
'Twixt twelve and one o'clock at night;
Your way around your chamber stealing,
O'er drawers and trunks, and toilets reeling;

All trembling, fearing, freezing, hoping,
In preparations for eloping!
I've known the thing gone through by dozens;
It happened to *my* four first cousins.

Determined ere her passions cool
To play the' irrevocable fool;
Just as the old ones turn their backs,
The fair her prettiest *jupons* packs;
Was never midnight sent so slow—
At length the lover stands below.
The letter on the toilet lies,
To wipe the household's morning eyes.
" Hope—anguish—duty—heart too tender—
She 's sure her mother would commend her—

Chance—fate—forgive her—or forget her,"
All know the true elopement letter.

She listens at the chamber-door,
But not a soul will deign to snore;
She trembles at the window's height,
The very moon seems up in spite.
Till safe on *terra firma* landed,
By Cupid and the lover handed;
Through man-traps, spring-guns, briers, and brambles,
The pair begin their marriage rambles.
Snug in the by-way stands the chaise,
Off go the spanking set of bays;
To Scotland turning all their noses,
That road being always strew'd with roses.

Till fagg'd, and frighted, starved, pursued—
By bar-maids envied, grooms halloo'd—
All dust, and heat, and smoke, and smother,
Already crop-sick of each other—
Yet for true penitents decreed,
They reach that Styx of Love—the Tweed.

For England's vulgar groves and lawns,
Now Scotia's landscape on them dawns;
Beside them steals the muddy rill—
Above them towers the naked hill;
Around them vegetates the hovel,
Where brutes, both two and four-legg'd, grovel;
And lassies gay, with scarlet locks,
All innocent of shoes and smocks.

Till shown in pity to their sighs,

The Smithy's sacred smokes arise;

Where shines the drunken son of Etna,

The high-priest of thy temple, Gretna.

Before him stand the culprits pale,

Dim, dusty, draggled head and tail:

The lady like a drooping lily,

'Twixt tear and smile, 'twixt sad and silly;

The man, a man, no matter what,

Love thinks too rapidly for *thought*.

Down goes the fee, on goes the ring,

The little Loves all clap the wing;

The fatal word 's by Vulcan spoken,

For which they 'll wish his neck were broken.

I reach the Rout, find every stair

A package of the fainting fair;

Find every inch of every room
Cover'd with petticoat and plume;
A group of the Fitz—— chins,
Rabbies might envy them their skins;
The H——gh, resistless figure,
The glass of fashion, *à la rigueur*.
No art of life can make a dance—
In vain my lord and lady prance;
The weary shufflers stand stock still,
Till dies the death, the choked quadrille.

Then turning off my cab to Boodle's,
I glance upon the high-born noodles,
That, silent as a ring of Quakers,
Melt their right honourable acres;
See the fat Viscount's heavy fist
Sweep thousands at two-handed whist;

While Verjuice, genius of the place,
Hunts, like a hound, his wither'd Grace;
And Owlface, ghost of other years,
Babbles the feats of long-past peers,
When ancient Queensberry shook the box,
And all men join'd to pigeon Fox.

Dear Gaming, if my easy rhyme
Shall ever reach the true sublime;
If ever from the Muse's rill
A drop within my plume distil,
That drop be sacred to thy praise,
Thou " Love" of noble nights and days!
Gaming! to thine, ecstatic witch,
Aladdin's wand was but a switch.
Let Katterfelto Hohenlohe,
Work miracles on tooth or toe;

Rescue from purgatory's fires
A nun's four bones, much more a friar's;
Give flesh and blood to wooden legs,
Teach Irish hens to lay fresh eggs:
Or cool the blood, or thin the skulls
Of patriots of the land of bulls;
Or bid old Nick make ropes of sand,—
You 'll beat his Highness out of hand.

Delightful work, to see the stroke
That shaves a province of its oak;
That, where the mighty mansion stood
A sort of heirloom of the flood,
That scorn'd the Dane's and Norman's spoil,
A thing imbedded in the soil;
Let but thy sceptre give a twist,
The walls are melted into mist;

The wooded hill, the teeming plain,
Are empty as their master's brain;
While go the lords of hills and valleys
To snuff the fishy gales of Calais;
Or reinforce thy sands, Boulogne,
With ragged leaders of the ton.

Or let it give another tweak,
The common, bleakest of the bleak,
Where not even gipsies make their den,
A sallow waste of weed and fen,
Some sullen solitude of sand,
Some second Bagshot of the land,
Where, but a highwayman, or *Duke*,
No man would give a second look;
Wave but thy cue, a palace rises,
A wood the native eye surprises;

A river through the meadows gushes,
You count the vine and peach by bushes;
Along the causeway's narrow'd border
A portal, Nash's native order:
Sublime whitewasher, great rough caster,
The Michael Angelo of plaster;
That, give him but his fling in brick,
Defies the Roman and the Greek;
Invites the passing stage-coach noses
To drink the otto of its roses.

While, deep its sacred bowers within
Shrined from the world's oppressive din,
Cool in the broad verandah's shade,
The hero of the scene is laid:
Around him shine the works of Buhl,
The living bronze, the gold pendule;

The Grecian group, the Tuscan vase,
The case of humming birds from Mawe's;
The Titian glowing from Madrid,
(A Monarch's self was there outbid;)
The Venus starting from her nest,
Not Lansdowne has her lighter drest.

Ye endless vineyards, for whose table
Wear ye all hues from white to sable?
Ye mighty orangeries, for whom,
Like ladies, lay ye on your bloom?
Ye groves of peach and plum, ye pineries,
For whom are worn your birth-day fineries?
Whose hand Patrician dares to cull ye?
Answer, ye perfumed breezes—Gulley!

Gaming! what charm of lip or eye
Can with thy thousand beauties vie?
From woman's glance, what living flash
Rivals the radiance of the cash?
Though woman's tongue in silver flows,
Yet gold 's the music of rouleaux.
Thou, that giv'st all the virtues scope,
The Hope, that to the last will hope;
The more than soldier's boasted Courage,
That goes to ruin without demurrage;
The Love, that makes our neighbour's pelf
As dear to all, as to himself;
The Loyalty that, live or die,
Still keeps the *Sovereign* in its eye.

L'ENVOY.

H—ll—d, now five fathom deep,
Send I politics to sleep,
Longing to enjoy a laugh
With thee and thy better half.
Where no literary bevy
Suffocate your evening levee
With their bald, disjointed chat,
Of who wrote this, and who stole that;

L'ENVOY.

Who scribbles in the next Review,
Whose wife's a brimstone or a blue;
Each with his own mysterious hint
Of *me, before* I dipp'd in print.
—" A poem, first-rate, high-life *tact;*
Sublime, yet every word a fact.
A most surprising show of νους,
They say, a leader in the house;
The principles so much the thing,
He dined last Sunday with the King."
Another sneers,—" The work's seditious,—
'Tis true the names are all fictitious;
But should his hits be thrown away,
The author's publishing a key!"
Another, more emphatic still,
A sort of quintessence of quill.

" The Author's name?—a thing forbidden,
From all particularly hidden.
A noble Lord has had the credit,—
'Twas said for certain, that he read it;
'Twas fasten'd on a travelled Duke,
Of *late* he has a *business look*.
A Bishop's whisper'd."—" *Entre nous*,
My Lord, the babe was given to you,
It has your wit, your brilliant style"—
"You make your answer by a smile."
" I know, the feeling of the *trade* is,
That, if not yours, it is my lady's."

The book has forty sires, at least.
As far from fact, as west from east.
Each marks his man—" A foreign prince,
(He fled the country ever since)

L'ENVOY.

Too poor, *he* says, to keep his **carriage**,
(I 'm sure, not beggar'd by his *marriage*.")
—" A minister, a noted wit,
Heir of the mantle dropt by **Pitt**."
—" A great commander."—" Right or **wrong**,
You 'll have the thing avow'd, ere long."
—" Two Chancellors, an in and out;
They wrote the couplets, turn about."
—" A most facetious reverend Dean,
Grown fat with work behind the screen."
—" A certain *very* stately Lord,
Much with Lord **Londonderry** bored."
Till sick of all the fools together,
You turn the talk on wind and weather;
Or seeing on your moveless dial
How drags like death your hour of trial,

O

Not bound to bear them (like a wife)
You fly to save your ears and life.

Let those who may, the secret tell,—
Now women—critics—world—farewell!

THE END.

LONDON:
PRINTED BY S. AND R. BENTLEY, DORSET STREET.

aaw

**PLEASE DO NOT REMOVE
CARDS OR SLIPS FROM THIS POCKET**

UNIVERSITY OF TORONTO LIBRARY

H&SS
A
6255

ImTheStory.com

Personalized Classic Books in many genre's

Unique gift for kids, partners, friends, colleagues

Customize:
- Character Names
- Upload your own front/back cover images (optional)
- Inscribe a personal message/dedication on the inside page (optional)

Customize many titles Including
- Alice in Wonderland
- Romeo and Juliet
- The Wizard of Oz
- A Christmas Carol
- Dracula
- Dr. Jekyll & Mr. Hyde
- And more...